ProcessWriting:
A Systematic Writing Strategy

STEPHEN D. GLADIS

Foreword by
Dr. Donald R. Gallehr
Co-Director of The National Writing Project

Published By
Human Resource Development Press, Inc.
    22 Amherst Road
    Amherst, Massachusetts 01002
    (413) 253-3488 (Mass.)
    1-800-822-2801 (outside Mass.)

ISBN 0-87425-093-5

First printing January, 1989

Printed in the United States of America. No part of the material should be reproduced or utilized in any form or by any means, electronic or mechanical, including photocopying, recording, or by information storage and retrieval system without written permission from the publisher.

DEDICATION

To Don Gallehr for being my mentor
and for teaching me about
the writing process.

TABLE OF CONTENTS

A Special Note to Teachers and Trainers	i
Preface	v
Foreword	xi
Acknowledgements	xiii

1. **SELECTING** — 1
   - Who — 3
   - Why — 4
   - When and Where — 6
   - What — 8
   - How — 8
   - ProcessWriting Workshop #1: Selecting — 10

2. **EXPLORING** — 17
   - Collecting — 19
   - Connecting — 20
   - ProcessWriting Workshop #2: Exploring — 24

3. **FASTWRITING** — 27
   - Freewriting — 30
   - Freelisting — 32
   - Webbing — 34
   - Freespeaking — 35
   - Preferences — 36
   - ProcessWriting Workshop #3: Fastwriting — 38

4. **SURVEYING** — 47
   - Reviewing What You've Written — 51
   - Finding Out What You Know — 53
   - Deciding What Works — 53
   - Discovering Connections — 55
   - Making a List of Key Words — 55
   - ProcessWriting Workshop #4: Surveying — 57

5.	HUNTING	63
	Interviewing Others	65
	Developing a Thesis Statement	68
	Where to Find Sources	70
	Interviewing Books	73
	Systematic Process	77
	ProcessWriting Workshop #5: Hunting	78
6.	WRITING	83
	Organizing Your Notes	85
	Refining the Thesis Statement	87
	Writing the Draft	88
	Reviewing the Draft	89
	ProcessWriting Workshop #6: Writing	91
7.	REVISING	97
	Scanning the Draft	99
	Developing Topic Sentences	101
	Making Transitions	103
	Pronouns	105
	Repeated Words and Synonyms	106
	Paragraph Length	107
	Communicating Your Ideas	107
	ProcessWriting Workshop #7: Revising	109
8.	REWRITING	115
	The Introduction	118
	The Body	121
	The Conclusion	124
	Structure to Stand On	125
	ProcessWriting Workshop #8: Rewriting	126
9.	TESTING	135
	The Writer–Broker Concept	137
	Writing Support Groups	138

The COACH Method	139
Expert Readers	143
ProcessWriting Workshop #9: Testing	145

10. ENDING — 149

Allow Time	151
Read Your Writing Aloud	151
Use the Active Voice	152
Avoid the Verb "Is"	153
Use Short Sentences—The Rule of Twenty	154
Don't Smother Verbs	155
Use Concrete Language	156
Keep Related Words Together	156
Determine Point of View	158
Make Your Writing Readable	159
Letting Go	160
ProcessWriting Workshop #10: Ending	161

A SPECIAL NOTE TO TEACHERS AND TRAINERS

General Description of Text

ProcessWriting: A Systematic Writing Strategy is a how-to-write book. Intended for the businessperson or the student, *ProcessWriting* can work well as a self-directed learning text or can form the basis for business in-service training. It can also serve as a supplemental text for a business writing course in a high school, technical school, college, or university. The book's primary purpose is to teach the writing process—a step-by-step method that takes the mystery out of writing.

The book covers the ten steps of ProcessWriting, from the development of the idea (exploring) to the final editing (ending). Each step builds on the previous one, and each chapter ends with a ProcessWriting Workshop. The Workshop consists of writing objectives and writing exercises for students, and it develops one specific memorandum report from chapter to chapter to illustrate the workshop steps of ProcessWriting.

How to Use the Text

The text is flexible. You can use it to review your own writing process, and you can recommend it to those students, who by virtue of their own particular schedules, must work alone. You can confidently use it as a training text in the classroom, on the high school, collegiate, and corporate levels.

The exercises at the end of the chapters are designed for hands-on instruction. They are direct and simple, but most effective in teaching the writing process. When I teach from this text, I assign the exercises both for in-class work and homework. The combination does two things: first, it shows the students that the exercises are worthwhile and, therefore, class time is allowed for them; second, it teaches the students how to use the text on their own.

I developed the ProcessWriting illustration as a modeling device—to show students what each step in the writing process might look like. I have found that when students can concretely visualize what an assignment is supposed to look like, their writing anxiety is reduced. The illustration is located at the very end of the chapters following the ProcessWriting exercises.

Those students who must work on their own can use the text without the oversight of an instructor. Because the steps are short and compartmentalized, students can easily complete the assignments and send them for review to a trainer for quick comment.

Teachers, trainers, and students will want to design their own courses, as their own needs dictate. However, I have used *ProcessWriting* with excellent results in a one-week format for in-service training. I ask that students come to the training with a particular piece of writing in mind. And I ask that the writing be important to them—and something they need to get done but for one reason or another haven't been able to complete. Thus, when they come to the classroom, they have something they *need* and *want* to complete. *ProcessWriting* works best, of course, when it provides immediate payback to the student. The one-week format concentrates instruction and provides an opportunity for lots of feedback. The final writing is due on the next to the last day of class. I use the last day for a wrap-up, individual writing conferences, for discussions on the process, and for a course critique.

Steve Gladis

PREFACE

As I write this book, I am forty years old—a baby boomer whose early education began in a Catholic grammar school. I learned the basics there: reading, writing, and arithmetic. But rather than tell you *what* I learned, I'd like to explain *how* I learned—particularly, how I learned to write.

I had a teacher, Sister Mary Immaculate Conception. Sister, like most teachers of her day, demanded that students know all the rules of spelling, punctuation, and grammar that govern the English language. With that jumble of rules balanced precariously in my mind, much of it slipping and crashing on the cerebrum's floor, I was expected to write the perfect sentence—one that had all the words spelled right, grammar correct, and penmanship perfect. I was rarely able to do that, and when I did not, Sister let me know.

I'm not criticizing Sister; rather, I wish to point out that her theory of writing, popular in her day, was a one-step process of writing. Such a process demands perfection and can produce—at least among us not-so-perfect people—a sense of failure. Such a theory, which demands perfection the first time, can eventually produce hesitant writers—afraid to put a pen on paper for fear of failure.

Let me confess that far from being perfect, I have a host of writing problems. The two that have plagued

PROCESSWRITING: A SYSTEMATIC WRITING STRATEGY

me since birth are spelling and penmanship. In fact, I have no respect for a person who can spell a word only one way—it shows a sad lack of imagination! And I've always had a problem with my penmanship. When I was young I didn't like the way my writing looked on paper, so I wrote as little as possible and it never improved. Many people suffer from these and other problems that inhibit their writing. What's the answer to such problems in a day when we want to be accurate, yet creative? ProcessWriting.

Realizing that writing is a multistepped process, rather than a do-or-die one-step proposition, takes away much of the anxiety people experience when they write. If I have this idea that Sister is looking over my shoulder like a judge waiting to pass the final sentence, how can I write creatively? After all, I might be hanged at a moment's notice. On the other hand, if I know I'll have some time to work through the process step by step, and I know I can keep Sister (the judge) from looking over my shoulder until I've finished the product, I certainly have more of a chance at success. ProcessWriting takes the pressure off exactness.

So, what is ProcessWriting? Simply put, it's writing in steps. It's breaking down writing into a series of definable steps and tackling one at a time. *Process-Writing: A Systematic Writing Strategy* will help reduce your writing anxiety and get you writing, because it divides writing into doable steps. I've broken down the process into ten manageable

INTRODUCTION

steps: selecting, exploring, fastwriting, surveying, hunting, writing, revising, rewriting, testing, and ending. Each step leads slowly and safely to the next. The end product will be every bit as perfect as the one Sister demanded. Yet *ProcessWriting* allows you, the writer, some fun along the way, while keeping Sister from looking over your shoulder, at least for a while.

This book consists of ten chapters, each with self-directed or group-centered assignments called "ProcessWriting Workshop," geared to take you from thinking about your idea to editing your final draft.

Chapter 1 looks at how you should prepare to write. Called "Selecting," this chapter explores the early decisions you must make before you write, and what questions you'll need to ask yourself to give your writing a focus. In the exercises at the end of this chapter you'll get the opportunity to practice Process-Writing.

Chapter 2, "Exploring," considers how your mind works, particularly how it works unconsciously. You'll examine the database you've collected in your own mind and determine how to access it. The chapter delves into collecting and connecting functions, and looks at how you as a writer can use both to your advantage before ever putting pen to paper.

Chapter 3, "Fastwriting," introduces you to four fastwriting techniques that let you put your ideas on paper quickly, thus helping to reduce your writing anxiety. This chapter treats the techniques of free-

PROCESSWRITING: A SYSTEMATIC WRITING STRATEGY

writing, brainstorming or freelisting, webbing, and finally, freespeaking, the newest of these techniques.

Chapter 4, "Surveying," teaches you how to scan your fastwritten draft for ideas. Surveying finds out what you know and don't know about your topic—it finds the holes in your writing. You'll take care of filling these holes in chapter 5.

Chapter 5, "Hunting," concerns itself with the techniques for gathering information from outside sources: people and written materials. You'll also learn how to develop the all-important thesis statement.

Chapter 6, "Writing," teaches you how to integrate your newly acquired information into your next draft.

Chapter 7, "Revising," provides you with the first critical look at your writing. You'll examine your writing structure carefully and prepare it for reader comprehension. In this chapter you'll learn how to write clear paragraphs and how to link them together.

Chapter 8, "Rewriting," helps you put your writing into a logical structure. You'll learn how to construct and integrate the introduction, body, and conclusion.

Chapter 9, "Testing," shows you how to use others to improve your writing. This chapter examines the writing-broker concept and the COACH system. Each will help you improve your writing by using the help of others.

Chapter 10, "Ending," provides handy clean-up editing tips so you can high-polish your writing.

Each chapter ends with a ProcessWriting Workshop—teaching objectives, writing exercises, and a single illustration, which runs throughout the book—that will help instructors and students alike to stay on track, whether working with a class or alone. If you follow the easy steps of *ProcessWriting*, you will find yourself with a polished piece of writing in short order.

FOREWORD

We know that a journey of a thousand miles begins with one step. We know that a fine meal must go through extensive preparation before it is served; yet, when it comes to writing, we expect to go from blank page to finished product just-like-that.

Where did we get this expectation? Mostly from seeing books and not writers. In school, until recently, we saw only published writings, not drafts or works in progress. In fact, in our younger years we may not have thought at all about where a book came from or how it was written.

Such conceptions of writing die hard. We expect to write first-draft-final letters, memos, and reports, and are discouraged when the boss returns them for revision. We wish it wouldn't take so long to write a simple business letter. Even worse, we become so anxious about writing that we procrastinate until the last minute when we no longer have time to make changes.

Few of us were fortunate enough to attend schools where teachers taught writing as a series of steps. If we had, we would have a much different view of writing. We can't change the past. We can, however, thanks to this book, go forward and learn how to write by following steps used by successful writers.

Steve Gladis has based *ProcessWriting: A Systematic Writing Strategy* on the latest research and scholarship, as well as on his own extensive experience in writing. His approach is practical and powerful. He deals with the writer as a person, with the workplace writing environment, and with writing itself. He draws examples from the world of work and offers writing strategies which recognize that to writers on the job, time is the number one restraint. His steps are easy to follow and solve the problems which arise from rushing into writing without knowing where we're headed.

Steve Gladis has made it possible for us to get there from here.

>Dr. Donald R. Gallehr
>Co-Director of the National Writing Project and Director of the Northern Virginia Writing Project at George Mason University

ACKNOWLEDGMENTS

To my wife Donna for her friendship, support, and love. To Ginny Field for her editing. To Pat Solley for her advice and wise counsel. To Georgia Adams for all her support over the years.

1. SELECTING

Writing is thinking on a piece of paper. But you don't have to pen words or pound a typewriter to write. Much of the writing process can be done in your head. Selecting, the first and very important step in Process-Writing, often takes place in the mind. Of course, sometimes, especially at work, you cannot "select" your topic. Instead, the boss tells you to write a memo; you have a report that's due; or your own need dictates a specific topic (for example, you might need to ask for more personnel). Any one of a hundred reasons can prevent you from selecting your topic. But thousands of times you *can* and *do* select your topic. Selecting involves asking yourself some familiar questions about your topic: Who? Why? When and where? What and how?

WHO

First, *who* is your audience? Targeting and profiling your audience helps you select an appropriate topic and writing style. For example, when you write to your boss about a new office policy, you may be much more formal than when you write to your employees about that same policy. Who will read your writing necessarily impacts on your writing. If, for instance, you think a critical eye will read your writing, you will write with formal precision. Consider the policeman who writes a report that a defense attorney will scrutinize later. His audience will be more than critical; they will be adversarial, actively seeking flaws. Thus, police writing must remain cold and factual—it should leave nothing to interpretation.

Writing to a tough audience, even an adversarial one, is difficult, but you can easily accomplish it by using a process of dilution. Don't direct early drafts to the boss or the defense attorney; rather, direct them to a sympathetic associate or a friend. After you get some preliminary reactions, you can tighten and improve your draft through revising and editing. We'll talk in depth about how to do this in later chapters.

WHY

Second, once you've decided *who,* ask yourself *why*? Why am I writing? What do I want the audience to do or think after they read my writing? Your purpose is the goal, the target of your writing. If, for instance, you want your audience to have an in-depth background on a topic—say, background for an annual shareholders' meeting—then give facts. Facts are the building blocks of informational writing. If, however, you want to persuade the reader, you must support those facts with reasons and evidence—the mortar that cements facts into a persuasive structure. If you want the boss to buy a new piece of equipment, you'll need to show why he should. Giving facts like the equipment's specs and stats might be good for background, but they alone will not persuade. Along with this supporting data, you must give the boss reasons that will logically persuade and so enhance your chances of getting what you want.

Before you begin writing, try the following technique. At the top of your paper write the word **purpose**. Now write, in one sentence, what you believe your purpose to be. For example: "The purpose of this memo is to provide management with in-depth background data on super widgets." Or, "The purpose of this report is to provide data and analysis to support the recommendation to buy a new widget press for the production plant." Each of these purpose statements focuses the writer and reader on the end product right from the start. Each provides a fixed frame of reference.

To illustrate how such a purpose line can work for the reader—as well as for you, the writer—consider the purpose of the following paragraph:

> The procedure is actually quite simple. First you arrange things into different groups. Of course, one pile may be sufficient depending on how much there is to do. If you have to go somewhere else due to lack of facilities, that is the next step; otherwise you are pretty well set. It is important not to overdo things. That is, it is better to do too few things at once than too many. In the short run this may not seem important, but complications can easily arise. A mistake can be expensive as well. At first the whole procedure will seem complicated. Soon, however, it will become just another facet of life. It is difficult to foresee any end to the necessity for this task in the immediate future, but then,

one can never tell. After the procedure is completed, one arranges the materials into different groups again. Then they can be put into their appropriate places. Eventually they will be used once more, and the whole cycle will then have to be repeated. However, that is part of life.*

OK, what's it about? About as clear as mud, you say? Now, reread the passage after reading the following purpose statement: "The purpose of this memo is to outline the proper procedure to do laundry." Make more sense now? Why? Because you, the reader, knew the purpose up front.

Purpose statements also help readers take quick action: to read, to delegate, or to disregard the writing. For example, you write to the boss: "The purpose of this memo is to provide the recipe for good Salisbury steak." While the boss might love a piece of steak, he'll likely route it to the company chef, who will actually do the cooking. The boss will taste the results later—not study the recipe now!

WHEN AND WHERE

Now, with who (audience) and why (purpose) firmly in mind, you need to think about the *when* and the *where*—the timing of the topic. Sometimes a topic will

---

* John D. Bransford and Marcia K. Johnson, "Consideration of Some Problems of Comprehension," in *Visual Information Processing,* ed. William G. Chase (New York: Academic Press, 1973), p. 400.

float, while other times it will sink. Political considerations always influence a piece of writing. What happened before your boss read the proposal? Did he see a big article in the morning newspaper that talked about how poorly widgets perform? If he did, you're going to need a most persuasive document to overcome this poor timing. Depending on your topic's importance, you may have to wait a few days, weeks, or even months before surfacing it. Not everything has to be written or submitted right now. Timing can be crucial to the success of any project.

To consider timing, ask yourself these questions: What does the reader think of this topic? Has anything recently happened that pertains to the topic? Is now the best time (Monday, Friday, vacation time, etc.) to bring up this topic?

The boss's schedule, need, or both can affect whether or not your memo gets his consideration. If the boss seems rushed, harried, or distracted, wait for a more relaxed time to hand over an important proposal. This policy helps eliminate the risk of an out-and-out no. As a reverse strategy, you might try running simple things through during his harried times to get a quick yes or no. Just consider the risks when you think about timing.

WHAT

Next in the selecting step, consider *what* you write. Remember to select a topic that interests you. When writers "own" (have vital interest in) their writing, they create a much better product. Compare a rented home to one that is owned. The difference is obvious. Ownership evokes a pride. If you have a personal investment in something, generally you'll work harder to do a better job. So too with writing.

Now, we all must write about things that aren't at the top of our ownership list. It's hard to feel a deep sense of ownership when you write a memo about vacation leave times for the department, unless, of course, you need to convince the boss to let you go. But other memos may mean a lot to you: new ideas for capital expansion, thoughts on new markets to explore, analyses of profitability. Further, if you, as a manager, instill a sense of ownership in subordinates, the quality of their writing will rise dramatically.

HOW

Finally, one often overlooked element of writing is the actual physical document. *How* something looks can be as important as who, why, when, where, and what you write.

The reader has certain structural expectations that you must meet. If you submit your writing in an unfamiliar or incorrect format, the reader may reject it immediately or quit before finishing the document.

To help you visualize how something should look, examine samples of previous memos and reports on the same topic. Don't copy the style if you find mediocre language, but do copy the format. It makes sense to meet the reader's expectations—to do so is part of being a good writer.

Good selecting involves considering who you're writing to (the audience), why you're writing (the purpose), when and where you're writing (timing), what you write about (personal interest), and how you package it (format).

PROCESSWRITING WORKSHOP
SELECTING #1

You can't learn how to write by reading about it. You've got to write to become better at the skill.

At work you often don't have the luxury of writing about what you want. However, now you'll get that chance.

You've probably had the urge to make a meaningful suggestion or express a long-held opinion about something. You may have wanted to inform, persuade, or inspire the boss, a peer, or a subordinate.

Choose a job-related topic you'd like to write about—something you can work with throughout this book—to refine and revise. If you're already writing something, you can work on that.

Objectives

1. To establish what the writer wants or needs to write about.
2. To articulate the reaction that the writer wants the reader to have to the writing.
3. To list audience personality traits and needs before the writing begins.

Activities
Step 1
Let your thoughts run wild. Pretend you're writing—freewriting—an informal note to a friend. Begin writing for ten minutes, using the following statement as a prompt: "I would like most to write to _____ (person) about...." Don't be afraid to take on your dream. It may be to tell the boss you've got a better way to build a mousetrap. For a start, write to more than one audience (boss, peers, and subordinates) about more than one idea. You're simply digging for a topic aimed at a potential audience. Take time and have fun.

Step 2
Underline or bracket the ideas that most appeal to you. Now, number them in the order of their priority, with "one" as the highest priority. Choose the idea that most appeals to you and that may have some impact on the company. Also consider the timing of your topic. Will it appeal to your reader at this time? Be sure the topic will lend itself to some substantial development.

Step 3
To determine your purpose in writing, ask yourself what you want the reader to know or do after reading your report. Try completing the following sentence:

"After reading my report, the reader should know or do the following...."

Step 4

Who will read this report? What are their educational backgrounds, economic statuses, relationships to you, interests in the topic, needs (power, control, etc.), immediate goals, personal problems?

Writing as quickly as you can for seven minutes, try to develop, as accurately as you can, a profile of your reader. If it will help, use the following prompt: "My reader is _____ (my peer, my boss, etc.), and this is what I know about him/her)...."

Step 5

Develop a writing process partner or two. Your partners can be friends, colleagues, or family members—people you can trust and whose opinions you value. You will use them to test your writing—to bounce ideas off. Discuss your audience needs with your writing process partners. Revise your descriptions to take their feedback into account.

Illustration

NOTE: To illustrate each step in the writing process, a single example will be developed and refined throughout the book. From idea conception to final editing, you'll see ProcessWriting principles demonstrated concretely and realistically.

Step 1: Digging for a Topic

I would most like to write to my boss about improving my department: I need space; I need computers; I need training; I need travel and funding.

I would like to write to my peers about the help I need from them on training executive groups—on joint research projects—and on developing a new integrated curriculum.

I would like to write to subordinates to tell them they should be innovative and seek advanced training—to ask them about their hopes and aspirations for the future and about their career development.

Step 2: Narrowing the Field

At this point I would underline and/or bracket the idea of computers and the idea about an integrated curriculum. I would probably end up choosing the one dealing with computers.

Step 3: Seeking a Response

After reading the report, the reader, my boss, should (1) know what the needs are for computer training, and (2) approve a step to perform a needs assessment, which will be developed by an outside consultant.

Step 4: Profiling the Audience

My reader is my boss and this is what I know about her. She is a forty-two-year-old woman who is very vocal and does not like to read lengthy or complex proposals. Rather, she is the kind of person who likes things short and to the point. I guess, then, some sort of synopsis with the recommendations up front in my proposal will help, because she doesn't want to spend a lot of time wading through rhetoric. But she does want the analysis done; so, I must have the analysis in there. Maybe some charts and/or graphics would help pull it together for her.

She is very experienced and an exceptional instructor; she has been in teaching her whole life; she likes new and innovative things as opposed to stock and staid things. She also likes to be in the forefront of things; *new* is the key word for her; *innovative* is a key word for her; words like that would be trigger words, so, I might want to include those in my document. She has a strong work ethic, and she is careful about effort, time, and cost. She is loyal to the organization and basically a very ethical person. She works hard and recognizes that effort in others. She used to be very anticomputer, but now that she has started using it herself a little, she seems to be more and more involved in the process and more accepting at least to its word-processing aspect; so, I might want to use that aspect as the basis for my proposal.

Step 5

Talked to Joe Schmo, a colleague of mine, and he said my boss had been impressed at a recent board meeting with integrated computer systems that were presented by an outside consultant.

2. EXPLORING

Once you've answered the important selecting questions, you've begun to "write"—even though your paper remains blank. Now what do you do? You need to explore what you've selected. Like selecting, exploring is a prewriting exercise, designed primarily to make you think. Remember, writing is thinking on paper. Therefore, a step in your writing process that allows for thinking is critical to good writing. This chapter examines how you collect and store information, as well as how to connect it.

COLLECTING

First, consider how much information you've collected over the years. If you are thirty-five years old, you've collected information for at least 36 years. You have read, talked, touched, tasted, smelled, heard, and seen a lot, piling up experiences, and you have stored this information deep within your brain. All these bits of information may not readily surface in your conscious brain, but they do float somewhere in that great reservoir: your subconscious.

For the sake of illustration, think of your brain as an iceberg, with only its tip jutting above the surface of the water. Below the surface lies a massive, unseen base. The portion above the waterline represents our conscious brain. Your subconscious is like the massive base below the water level—out of sight, but ever present. It is this subconscious that stores so many collected ideas, some more deeply than others.

The ideas come flooding in daily, especially in this age of information. TV, radio, newspapers, and computers, simply increase the flood. You are at least vaguely familiar with an enormous range of topics because in today's society you cannot avoid being bombarded with information.

For example, let's say you want to hire a new assistant for your office to help increase its efficiency. Should you run down the street to the library, or should you call in an efficiency expert? Again, remember the iceberg analogy. You've been part of the office for years, collecting enormous amounts of information. Why not begin with what you know, because you probably know as much as anyone else about this topic. In fact, you'll find that when you do hire consultants in such a situation, they spend a lot of time asking you what you know. When they've finished their evaluation, the results should not shock you. Usually, they simply *write down what you know*. So, in the exploring step you just act like a consultant and think about what you know. Probe your subconscious and put your findings on a piece of paper.

CONNECTING

How do you get started? First, you must understand the process called connecting. You've been collecting information for years. Connecting simply allows you to pull together all the pieces of this information. If you can only vaguely remember collecting information on a topic, you must give yourself time to let the stimulus of the project or topic rattle around in your subconscious. This time allows you to connect bits of information collected in 1964 with bits collected three days ago. Time allows your brain to assemble a readout, much like that produced by a random search of a computer database. You input the topic, with the necessary parameters, and wait as your brain whirs, blinks, and connects. But you need to allow this process time.

How much time? The answer depends on each situation, because sometimes you don't have time. The boss calls, tells you to write something, and you must react immediately. When you have only a couple of hours or a day to get a memo out, apportion part of that time for some subconscious thinking. Write the idea on a card and place it on your desk. Go out for a walk; talk with a friend; go out for lunch—all the time you'll be thinking and mentally writing. You'll be exploring.

But what about those many instances when you do have time? When you've got the chance, try "sleeping on it" (the idea). This will help enormously. Again, help yourself by writing the topic down on a three-by-five card and propping it on your desk. Casual glances during the day will continue to stimulate subconscious as well as conscious thoughts on the topic. Each time your mind receives this visual stimulus, it will perform a kind of minisearch and research.

But remember, you must not allow so much time for exploring that you begin to procrastinate. Indefinitely putting off writing becomes counterproductive. Two weeks of stacking and reshuffling notes is procrastination, which does you no good. Your brain usually needs only a day for connecting.

With time to probe the subconscious, you'll experience a kind of thermodynamic phenomenon. Suddenly, ideas will begin to rise from the depths of the subconscious to the surface of the conscious. First they simmer; then they bubble; and before long, they boil. You will know when you've reached this rolling-boil stage. You'll begin to mumble, even talk to yourself. Your conscious mind will become intrigued by the idea, and you'll find yourself constantly drifting back to it. This phenomenon is a sure sign that you're preparing to write.

Next, you may even begin to feel anxious, uneasy. Your mind is seeking to organize its random thoughts and is calling on you to nail them down in concrete terms—with words. Once you put our ideas on paper, you'll be able to order and clarify them.

Many have written about writing apprehension or "writer's block." But you should understand that a certain amount of anxiety about writing is a normal and useful stimulus to writing.

That is not to say that some writers don't get blocked. However, most blockage comes from not knowing how to get from the exploring—prewriting—

stage to the writing stage. The next chapter shows you how to overcome writer's block by using fast-writing techniques to get ideas on paper quickly.

PROCESSWRITING WORKSHOP
EXPLORING #2

Not all writing takes place with a pen and a piece of paper or while sitting at a typewriter. Some of the writing process takes place in your head while you are sitting, walking, or driving. Allow time for your ideas to bubble to the surface.

Objectives

1. To show how time helps mature an idea.
2. To demonstrate the process of mentally exploring a topic.

Activities

Step 1

Take the topic you developed in chapter 1 and write it out in big letters on several index cards. Put one on your desk and another in your car, or wherever you plan to spend time in the next day or two.

Step 2

Now, go about your daily business, occasionally glancing at the cards.

Step 3

If you want to write an idea or two on the card, OK. Just don't write too much yet. When you get jittery, even antsy, you're getting ready to write—and you will in the next chapter, so hold on.

Illustration

Step 1: Focusing the Subject

> Computers in Training

Step 2: Thinking about the Topic

> THINK!

Step 3: Jotting Down Ideas

> **Computers in Training**
> Lesson Plans
> Objectives
> Database
> Word Processing

3. FASTWRITING

After mentally exploring a topic, you—like all writers—face a critical point in the writing process: physically beginning to write. Writers will do just about anything to avoid writing, from cleaning out briefcases and desktop drawers to sharpening pencils and rereading an article. And even when they do get started, you can hear the untimely crumple of paper and the snap of pencils as writers are struck by writer's block—the unmistakable ogre of hesitation and anxiety that often rears itself precisely at this point during the writing process.

But never fear, there are several solutions to the inevitable blockage in your path to writing. Here's the story of how one doctoral student solved his case of writer's block. This student had to finish his dissertation by a particular date or be forever a member of the ABD ("all but dissertation") Club, a club populated by many doctoral students who completed all the course work for the degree but who could never get over writer's block in time to finish the project.

This student was at a standstill, a major stall, in his writing and consequently went to a psychologist. After hearing the student's story, the savvy psychologist asked him how much money he had in the bank. The student replied, "$3,500."

"Fine," replied the psychologist. "Make me out a check for the entire amount. I will not cash it until one day after your dissertation is due, and only if you do not meet the deadline. If you do finish on time, you get the check back—except, of course, for my fee."

Bewildered but desperate, the student gave the check to the psychologist. Several months later, he successfully completed his dissertation and retrieved his check less, of course, a hefty fee.

This is one solution to writer's block, but it's potentially a bit more costly than most of us care to risk. As good alternatives, I suggest four fastwriting techniques, which have been developed from practice and research, that will be just as effective as the psychologist's method.

FREEWRITING

One of the most widely used techniques to get ideas on paper quickly and effortlessly is called freewriting. Like its name, freewriting relies on a liberated mind, much like the state of mind you may have when writing a letter to a trusted friend.

When freewriting, as when writing to a friend, don't worry about the mechanics of writing, only the ideas. Thus, you won't get bogged down in the details of grammar, punctuation, and spelling while producing an initial draft. The technique is quite simple: just put pen to paper and write as if you were telling a story.

It's important to pretend you're writing to a good friend because research has found that an overdeveloped sense of audience (that is, an intimidating audience, like the supervisor or chairman of the board) can cause writer's block and stop the writing process before it ever begins. Just remember the last time you had to write a letter to, or even worse, for the boss. If you're like so many others, you found yourself scratching out the words, stopping and starting, and generally spending an enormous amount of time writing. By mentally assuming the initial audience to be a good friend, you remove the judgelike authority figure in your mind. And guess what the results are? Yes, fastwriting. Certainly, it's a lot easier to write a memo to your old friend Jack or Jean than for the chairman of the board so why not freewrite the first draft to a friend?

The rules for freewriting are simple:

1. Choose your favorite pen, paper, chair, and place to write—they all make a difference.
2. Imagine a good friend, one who knows that you can't spell all the words in the dictionary and who knows you don't know all the grammar rules in the world—someone who won't prejudge you.
3. Start writing to your friend (Dear Jean) and don't stop for anything until you have explained your ideas in everyday language.
4. Don't correct spelling, punctuation, or grammar. Just let the pen roll out the ideas.

Freewriting is like priming a pump: it gets the ideas flowing. And with those ideas comes language. By selecting a nonthreatening audience, thinking and expressing your thoughts become easier and quicker. Freewriting unleashes the power of your brain by removing the anxiety that locked it there in the first place. To practice freewriting, simply sit down and write two or three letters to friends you haven't corresponded with in a while. Indeed, letter writing is the purest form of freewriting.

FREELISTING

Just as some people don't like to write letters, so too some people don't like freewriting. Don't worry, try freelisting—a way of self-brainstorming. Let's say you have to write a report and you just don't know where to begin (sound familiar?). Simply list the main topic at the top of a blank sheet of paper. Spray the page with related ideas; don't worry about their order and, whatever you do, don't laugh at your own ideas because some of the wildest ones may end up being the best. Then, step back, look at each idea and place it on a separate piece of paper or file card. Focus on brainstorming again on the single idea on that page. You're beginning to break down the component ideas and, in a very informal and free way, you're forming the basis for a working outline.

For example, let's try the topic of public affairs. Let's freelist about public affairs:

   Press relations
   Publications
   Speeches
   Correspondence
   Research

Now let's take one component idea—press relations—and break it down:

   Press conferences
   Liaison
   Press releases
   News inquiries

The process goes on until you cannot break each down any further. Let's look at some of the steps for freelisting:

1. Sit down at a favorite place with a favorite pen. Get comfortable.
2. Write the main topic at the top of the page and simply free-associate any ideas that come into your head and write them down as quickly as you can.
3. Step back from your original list and try to check off the main ideas. You'll find that some insignificant ones have been listed with the main ideas. Don't worry, the concept is to filter nothing out initially, simply to get the ideas flowing.

4. List each main idea on a separate sheet of paper or index card and repeat the brainstorming and freelisting for those subtopics.
5. Repeat the process until you can no longer break down your subideas.

Freelisting provides you with the basic ideas, even the foundation for an initial outline. It can be done quickly, alone, and anywhere—on a matchbook cover, a cocktail napkin, or on a scrap piece of newspaper.

WEBBING

This third fastwriting technique will appeal to those who are visual. Like its name indicates, webbing is a way of weaving your ideas together much as a spider would do. You spin your web by writing the main topic in the middle of a page and circling the word. Next you draw out lines to bubbles of ideas that relate to the main ideas. Pretty soon you've developed a weblike sketch on your paper. You'll easily see where you need more research and where your ideas are highly developed. More importantly, you'll be able to "see" your report, to visualize your writing.

Let's try an example to see how it works. We'll explore the topic of corporate fitness programs:

Quickly, you can see a piece of writing taking shape. This piece, in fact, might whip the entire company into shape.

Let's review the webbing steps:
1. Don't think about any particular audience.
2. Write your main topic in the middle of the page.
3. Draw lines off the central topic to related ideas.
4. Continue to break down subideas by drawing off lines to related subideas until you can spin your web no further.

5. Step back from your web and reinspect it with a fresh eye.

FREESPEAKING

The last fastwriting technique will appeal to people with a good ear. If you've ever said, "I'm just thinking out loud," or "I'm just talking to hear myself think," then you've already experienced freespeaking.

Freespeaking is similar to dictation, but it flows more freely. To freespeak you need to use a tape recorder and pretend you're talking to someone—a specific audience, a trusted friend. This technique allows you to discuss your ideas with an audience and to develop and analyze them as you talk. The initial words may come out awkwardly, but after a sentence or two, the speaker who is comfortable with speaking skills will in no time roll out ideas and create a draft. For obvious reasons, this technique seems to appeal to people who like to talk. Again, keep your tone conversational; you need impress no one.

You should freespeak until you finish your piece. Usually it takes no more than ten minutes to produce a ten-page, typewritten document. When you finish freespeaking, transcribe what you've "written." I suggest transcribing the recording *exactly* so you can get the richness of your spoken language into your written language. Then be prepared to make major revisions to make your message clear to others. This technique takes advantage of the strongly practiced speaking skills we all generally possess; it uses them to produce the foundation of the written piece. The disadvantage of this technique is that spoken drafts often contain a great deal of repetition. Thus, they require a lot of editing.

Here's a brief review of freespeaking:
1. Set up a tape recorder in a quiet room.
2. Assume a trusted friend as your audience.
3. Speak freely in a conversational way.
4. Transcribe your tape recording.

PREFERENCES

Remember the old saying, "Different horses for different courses"? Well, that saying applies especially in fastwriting techniques. What works well for one person may not work well for another. Some people are holistic and prefer freewriting. Others are analytical and prefer freelisting. Some are visual and prefer webbing. And others are aural and prefer freespeaking.

Each of these fastwriting techniques will appeal to different people While no one technique necessarily outshines the others, all offer a place to start writing. They free the mind's ideas and get them on paper—a critical event since creating the "raw material" often causes writers great anxiety. By using these ideas, as others have, the power of writing quickly and with enjoyment will be yours.

PROCESSWRITING WORKSHOP
FASTWRITING #3

Staring at a blank page intimidates even the most experienced writers. But several techniques can help you break through "writer's block" and get your words flowing on paper. Once you've tried each of these, you may find one that you prefer. At first, however, try them all.

Objectives

1. To develop a discovery draft to find out what you know about your topic.
2. To help relieve writer anxiety.
3. To discover the creative force of writing.

Activities

Step 1: Freewriting

Choose any topic on your list, other than the one you've selected for your report, and freewrite about it as though you were writing a letter to a friend. Freewrite for about 10 minutes. Remember, don't stop and don't worry about punctuation, spelling, or grammar. Just write.

Step 2: Brainstorming/Freelisting

Select another topic. Now, break it down into some main headings. Break down those headings further, then break those subheads further into sub-subheads, etc., until you can't break them down any more. Work on this exercise for 10 minutes. Does an outline begin to emerge for you?

Step 3: Webbing

Select another topic. This time use the webbing technique to form a map. Write your topic in the middle of a page and draw connecting boxes or bubbles of subtopics to it. Again, as you did while brainstorming, keep breaking down headings to form a picture of your paper. Take 10 minutes to do this exercise.

Step 4: Freespeaking

Select a fourth and final topic. Now, simply give your writing-process partner some paper and a pen and begin to talk freely about your topic. Your partner should listen and take notes. Keep talking for five minutes. This exercise works even better with tape recorders. If you have one available, use it; then, simply transcribe your freespeaking to serve as a discovery draft.

Step 5: Evaluation and Discovery Draft

Now that you've had the chance to try each technique with a different topic, you may find that you prefer one method of fastwriting over the others. Decide which technique you like the most and use it on the topic you've selected for your report. This fastwriting draft will serve as a discovery draft and the starting point for your paper.

Illustration

NOTE: To demonstrate clearly the different characters of the fastwriting techniques, I will use only one topic, **Computers in Training**, to illustrate the steps.

Step 1: Freewriting

Dear Joe,

I'm writing you this letter because I need a friendly ear to listen to my idea. I feel pretty stupid because I know I won't be actually mailing this thing to you. So here goes. As you know, I'm the training coordinator for our company, and a large part of my job centers on teaching executives to speak and write. Now, mind you, they're all pretty articulate, but my job is to help them polish any rough edges—through a training program.

My work would be tremendously enhanced if I were able to purchase some computers. To refresh your memory, I've got six instructors who report to me. I require each of them to have a lesson plan on file for each of their blocks of instruction. The tough part, Joe, is that we've only got one secretary—mine—for all of

us users. It's impossible for her to keep up. Thus, we have a lot of classes for which we have no lesson plans on file. This creates tremendous problems when someone is sick or transfers out of the group.
I thought if we could get these computers it would help take the pressure off the secretary and give the instructors a good assist....

Step 2: Freelisting

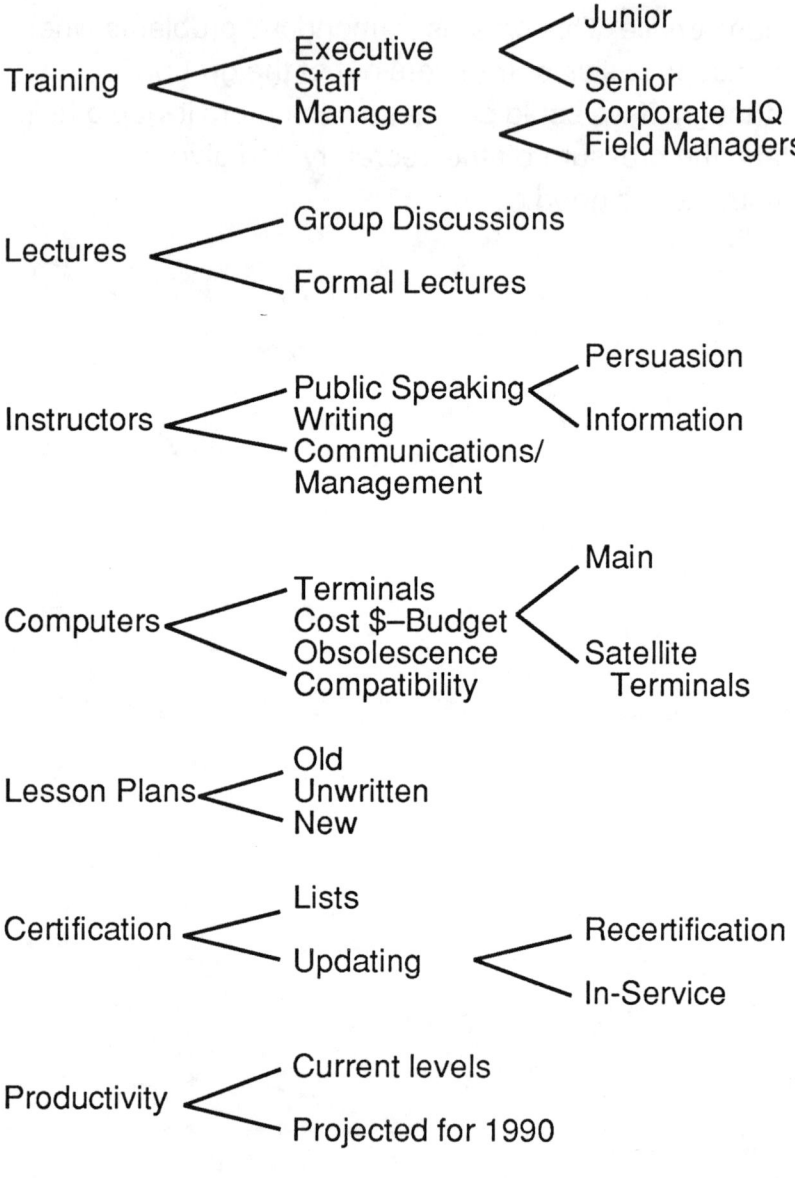

Step 3: Webbing

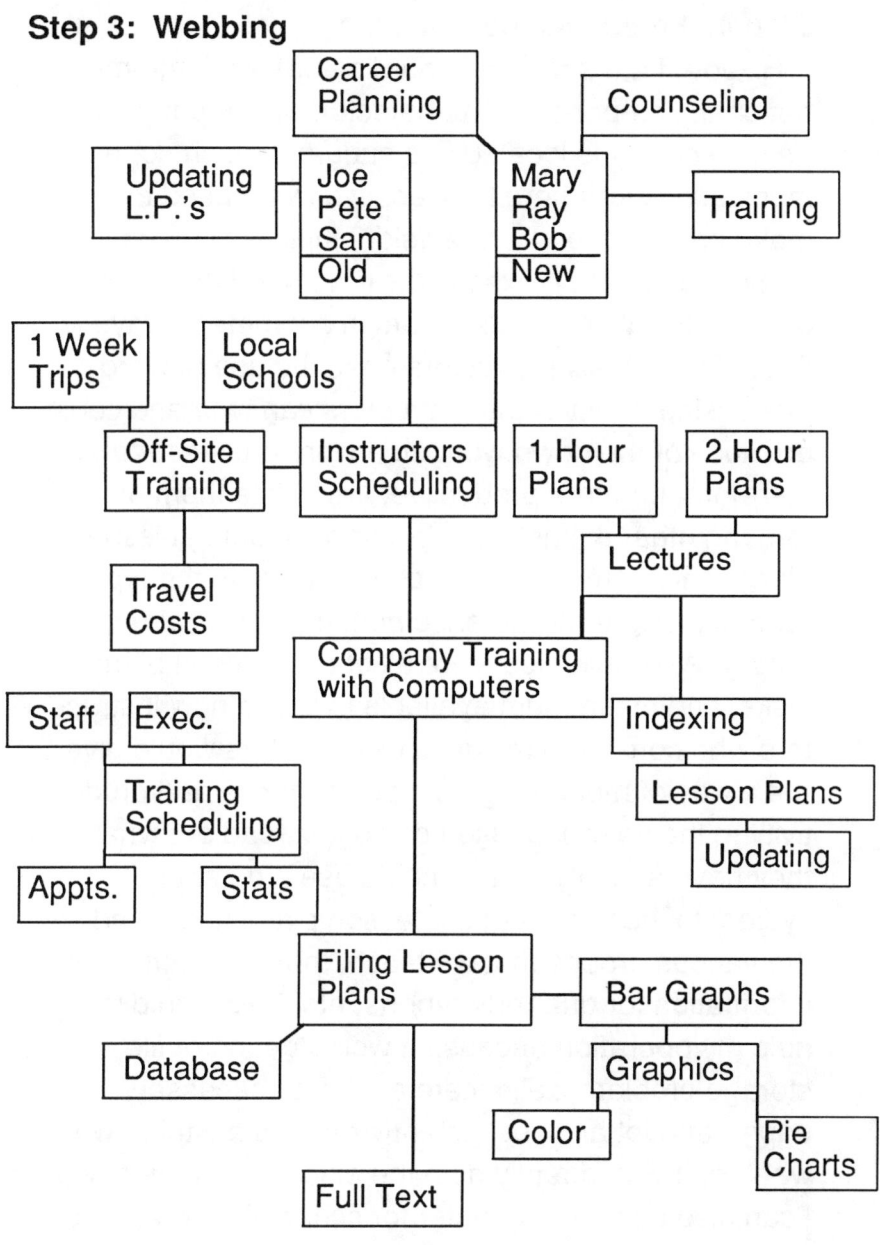

Step 4: Freespeaking

Hi, Joe, I am a training coordinator for a large multinational ping-pong ball manufacturing company. Our training center is located in a suburb. I teach communication skills here to executives who need to make presentations in the field. I think we could do a better job for these executives if we had computers in our facility. We could use them in a variety of ways. First of all, my six instructors need the use of word processing. Most of the instructors can type and could do much of their own work on a word processor and, therefore, be more productive. I evaluate them on (among other things) writing and developing lesson plans. The word processor could eliminate the typing burden and greatly increase both their skills and their output. We could also store all of their lesson plans on disks, and make them available to brand new instructors who come into my group. Computers would give *me* a way of measuring their performance and productivity in the year because I could just read out what they have actually done. I could use a database system to index a lot of the lesson plans and to index the various groups that we teach, then just retrieve the information for quarterly reports, etc. This would really help my operation because it would get rid of file storage problems, eliminate a lot of unnecessary paper, and let all of us instantly retrieve anything we wanted. It would really help the efficiency of the office. I can also use the computer for scheduling. My office needs a lot of scheduling to keep it running efficiently. Right now it's being done by hand—it's inefficient—and there are software packages out that could solve the whole problem. I could get a report on the status of anything I wanted, like program progress in the office. I don't know much about this kind of equipment—the type of technical equipment out there or even how much it costs—but I do know there are ABC computers and XYZ computers available that might be good. I'll have to find out more about the equipment and its capabilities before I can actually recommend a specific type to my boss, but my inclination is to go with ABC's because they've been around, they're in more companies, and they're more compatible industrywide. Again, I don't know all that much about it. Maybe XYZ computers might be better because they have more education and training software. Right now, though, I think we should go for an in-house loop that would be ABC compatible and would be compatible with the machines that we have in our district offices.

4. SURVEYING

SURVEYING

By now the worst is over. You've overcome any incipient writer's block by getting your first words down on paper. You've already come a long way! You've selected a topic, explored it in your mind, and scrawled what you know about it. That's more than most people do. Most just talk about what they're going to write. How many times have you heard people say, "Someday I'm going to write a book"? But how many even get close to starting? Until they commit something to paper—begin the writing process—nothing will happen, least of all a book manuscript. So, congratulations for getting farther than most. But what now? What do you do with your scores of discursive phrases, lists, and sentences?

The next step in the writing process is called surveying. Surveying requires just what it says: to examine what you've written to find out what you know about the topic, to learn what works, and to discover new connections.

Let's say you've just freewritten 10 pages proposing that your company merge with XYZ Corporation. Many fellow employees would not even dare to think about such a wild idea, but you've dared to write about it. OK. There they are on paper, the ramblings of a wildman, your thoughts in a jumble of words, phrases, and sentences that make sense to you alone. How do you refine your ideas so someone else can read and understand them, even accept and act on them? Surveying is the answer.

When you allow yourself to let ideas flow wildly and creatively, you open the floodgates to torrents of possibilities. Unfortunately, you also allow lots of unnecessary words to wash in. Often only you can penetrate the wordiness, so if you want others to understand and act on your ideas, you must clarify them. Surveying does just that. Quite simply, Surveying forces you to look over your fastwriting or scrawling for the big picture, for the developing trends—for the potential of your ideas.

Surveying is much like buying an older home as an investment. When you walk in the front door, it nearly falls off its hinges; the floors creak; and the banister dangles by a few screws. A lesser person might run, but the entrepreneur sees potential. Entrepreneurs see the original oak doors, the sturdy maple banisters bolstered by white bleached birch spindles, and the parquet floors. Why? Because they survey that old house with an eye for potential.

So, how do you survey your writing for potential? Just like the entrepreneurs do in that old house, by looking around and grouping things into categories. Most minds don't produce ideas in neat packages. Rather, free-floating ideas fill your mind, waiting to connect with something in your life or in your writing. In fact, that's what makes writing so much fun. It allows you to make new connections, ones you didn't know existed until you put them together on paper.

In this chapter you'll learn the steps in surveying: reviewing what you've written, finding out what you know, deciding what works, discovering connections, and making a list of key words.

REVIEWING WHAT YOU'VE WRITTEN

A few hours or days after the fastwriting step, read through your draft quickly to get a sense of what you've written. By allowing time between fastwriting and surveying, your reading will be much more objective, less subjective—much more readerlike, less ownerlike.

Now, read through the draft again, but this time ask yourself what ideas dominate the draft, what ideas can link with others? Many writers call the first scribbled draft a zero-base draft because its ideas lead directly to the first draft. Thus, the zero-base draft is an idea draft. Surveying helps you begin to organize and group your written ideas into an intelligible whole.

As you survey your draft for potential, use a yellow highlighter to underline similar ideas. The highlighter provides a broad sweep of the pen, exactly what you're looking for in this draft—sweeps of ideas.

Once you've swept through the draft, go back over and number or letter your ideas. For example, while sweeping through your draft, you might find an idea A on page one, with one related bit of information on page three, and yet another on page twelve. By lettering (or numbering) your ideas, you can locate

PROCESSWRITING: A SYSTEMATIC WRITING STRATEGY

and group apples with apples and oranges with oranges. This should help you decide how to construct your paper.

For instance, you're writing about a new detergent that you think your laundry company should use. Let's look at how you might begin surveying. First, you've freewritten a memo to your boss about the advantages of switching detergents, and ended up with pages of fastwriting. Next, you go over your memo, highlighter in hand, and on page two you discover your first good idea: the old product has increased in price by 13 percent over the last year. Label this idea A. While proceeding with your survey, you see another idea: increased customer complaints about spots staying in soiled shirts. Label this idea B. Further on, you find an idea on customers complaining about the ten cent increase in price for starching dress shirts—another A idea. As you proceed with surveying the draft, the labeled ideas suddenly will present you with a road map of where to go.

Remember, most people don't think in nice straight lines, and your thoughts probably will not be immediately expressed in neat categories. You need surveying to help you recognize similar ideas so you can make organizational decisions.

What about the material you've left unhighlighted? Forget it. It's extraneous, the writer's equivalent to the film on the film editor's cutting room floor. You must mentally clip it off, forget it, and move on.

FINDING OUT WHAT YOU KNOW

An immediate benefit of surveying is to find out what you know about a topic. Surveying, though sometimes humbling, can often encourage you. Most of the time you will finish your survey while saying to yourself, "Great! I know a lot more than I thought about widgets." By spreading the draft in front of you and reviewing it for ideas, you gain confidence.

While surveying, you probably will find at least one gaping hole in the middle of your writing. For example, while surveying your writing about new software for your company's computers you discover the words **intercomputer compatibility,** but you have only that phrase to highlight. You've just uncovered a good idea, but it seems to need some research. In finding out what you don't know, you have given yourself a lead for the future.

DECIDING WHAT WORKS

At this point, you are making only temporary decisions. Surveying helps you tentatively decide what will work and what will not. Only when you've read what you've written can you decide what works or fails to work. Thinking and writing are close cousins, but they're not the same—no more so than writing and talking.

Remember, your thoughts may make perfect sense to you—you've got a particular mindset and base of information—but you can't assume they will make sense to your readers. You can't assume your readers know everything you do. Thus, you also have to survey the validity of your thoughts on paper. What "thinks" well does not necessarily "write" well, at least the first time, so you need to survey.

While surveying, you might find some well-formed ideas, nearly perfect for reader consumption. These often are old ideas that you've rethought and revised for years. However, you may also find germs of ideas, and these first-time thoughts are often ill-formed and imperfect. Such first-generation ideas, as opposed to tenth-generation thoughts, will require more scrutiny and revision.

Thus, you'll have to choose the ideas that will work the best. How good are the germ ideas? Are they worth more work, or are they just fleeting thoughts that should be left behind? Because you've written them down, you can focus on their individual worth, which is difficult to do when you're trying to hold a welter of ideas in your mind simultaneously.

DISCOVERING CONNECTIONS

Connections are as important in writing as they are in thinking. In chapter 2 we looked at connections in the thinking stages of writing. Your mind constantly makes connections or associations: someone on the train to work reminds you of cousin Ed; a billboard advertising skin lotion shows a mountain scene, and you think of your trip to Vail last year. Your brain makes connections all the time, and through these connections you construct and view the world. It's the new connections you make among ideas that gives life and vitality to your writing.

MAKING A LIST OF KEY WORDS

Finally, after you've highlighted the key ideas in your zero-base draft, list them on a separate piece of paper. If you put all the A's together, then all the B's, and so on, this list will become your working outline, your stepping-stone to the next stage of writing. Does that mean you must stick to this initial list? No. You'll revise this working outline as you continue to collect new ideas and information. It simply gives you a base on which to start adding new information or from which to slice away old, unworkable ideas.

Surveying forces you to review and account for what you've written and to begin structuring your writing. Notice that before surveying you spent most of the time *producing* ideas. Now, you have practiced *choosing* among them.

Surveying gives you a beginning inventory of idea categories, and when you categorize them you can organize them, if only on a rudimentary level. From this point, you must decide how detailed you want to make the levels of your categories. How and what levels of information you add to these categories comes with the next step in the writing process: hunting.

Your key idea list (outline) will help you with hunting. You will use it as a shopping list when you turn to other sources. But it won't restrict you: if you find something you need in the store that's not on the list, you simply add it.

PROCESSWRITING WORKSHOP
SURVEYING #4

Once you've gotten your thoughts about a topic on paper, you're ready to survey. Look for holes in your information—places in your fastwriting that seem to lack depth or substance. Surveying will help prepare you for the hunting phase.

Objectives

1. To clear away the clutter of the initial draft.
2. To discover what the writer does and does not know about the topic.

Activities

Step 1
Review your discovery draft on a grand scale. Label similar groups of ideas with the same letter or number to help you establish how much information you have in each main area.

Step 2
Review your groupings and list the areas that need more research or development.

Step 3

Underline or highlight the key words in your draft. Further, mark those words that seem essential or critically related to your topic.

Step 4

Now, list your key words and phrases on a separate sheet of paper. This paper will be your working outline. A working outline is a mushy and flexible thing. It gives tentative direction, so don't see it as your final outline—don't think you have to stick with it. Quite the contrary: you'll revise your working outline constantly as you pore over the research.

Illustration

NOTE: We'll use the freespeaking draft from chapter 3 in this series of examples:

Step 1: Review the Draft
Dear Joe,

   I am a training coordinator for our company. This company is a large multinational ping pong ball manufacturing company with a substantial training center located in a suburban area. My job is to [A]*teach communication skills* to executives who will be going out to the field for different reasons. In delivering our programs to various executive groups it has become evident that we are no longer capable of doing as good a job as we could do with the use of computers. I see the use of computers enhancing my operation in several different ways. First of all, in the use of [B]*word processing* for each one of my six instructors. Most of the instructors can type and could do much of their own work on a [B]*word processor* and, therefore, be more productive. I evaluate them on (among other things) writing and developing lesson plans. The [B]*word processor* could eliminate the typing burden and greatly increase their skills and their output in this particular area. We could also [C]*store* all of their lesson plans on disks, which could then be available to brand-new instructors who come into my group. Computers would give me a way of measuring their performance and ^D*productivity* in the year very quickly by reading out what they have actually done. I could use a ^C*database system* to index a lot of the lesson plans, and to index the various groups that we teach for retrieval. This could be used for reports that have to be done and for a variety of purposes. This would really help my operation because it would ^C*eliminate file storage problems*, eliminate a lot of need for hard copy, and would give me and the instructors instant retrieval when I or they need it. It would really help the efficiency of the office. I can also use the computer for ^E*scheduling*. My office needs a lot of scheduling to keep it running efficiently. Right now it's being done by hand and it's inefficient, and there are software packages out that could solve the whole problem. I could get a report on the status of anything I want, program progress in the office, and what we're doing. It's the ^F*kind of equipment* that I don't know much about—the type of technical equipment out there or even how much it costs—but I do know there are ^F*ABC computers* and ^F*XYZ computers* available that I know something about, although I need to know more about the equipment and its capabilities before I can actually recommend a specific type to my boss. My inclination is to go with ABC because they're more compatible industrywide. Again, I don't know all that much about it. Maybe XYZ computers might be better because they have more education and training software. Right now, though, I think we should go for an in-house loop that would be ᶠ*ABC compatible* and would be compatible with the machines that we have in our district offices.

Step 2: List Ideas Needing More Research
    Kind of equipment
    (Automated) Scheduling systems
    Database system

Step 3: Highlight Key Words
    See emphasis in step 1 example

Step 4: List Key Words
    Training
    Lesson plans
    Word processing
    Database
    Communication skills
    Productivity
    Scheduling system
    ABC Computer Company
    XYZ Computer Company
    Performance
    Storage
    Retrieval
    Costs

5. HUNTING

In the previous chapter, surveying, you discovered what you do and don't know about your writing topic. Now you must take the time to close your knowledge gaps—time to go hunting. If you were to ask someone where to go for information, what do you think most people, particularly students, would say? If you guessed the library or the company files, you're right, but they're wrong! You're right because that is what most students would say, but they're wrong because that's not the quickest way to begin the process of hunting for information.

In this chapter you will learn the hunting process: the way you can fill in gaps with information that will support your overall ideas. Specifically, you'll learn how to gather information from interviews, how to develop a thesis statement, where to find sources, how to "interview" a book or periodical, and how to take notes using notecards or notesheets.

INTERVIEWING OTHERS

By far the most overlooked, yet most helpful source of information is other people. In a sense, the process of hunting—whether for a company report, a school paper, or a civic club report—mirrors the modus operandi of a detective. Where do you begin? To answer this question you must first ask yourself what, in general, you want to know. If, for instance, you want to learn more about how to obtain computer technology for your new office, you need to think like a detective and to list on paper where you would find your most logical leads.

First, you might consider someone in your company who recently went through the same kind of search. Why reinvent the wheel? If someone else just did something similar to what you want to do, presumably that person had to go through the same steps you'd have to follow. He or she probably already made all the false starts and mistakes along the way that you would make. Therefore, that person should be able to help you take the most direct route to success. In short, don't overlook human resources in favor of written ones.

Second, if you are a new employee, you may want to interview the person whose job you filled. Unless disgruntled, your predecessor can give you a valuable historical perspective. Remember, you can place a real premium on experience, and learning from that experience for the price of a phone call, even a long-distance one, is valuable.

Third, look to experts to tell you where to look next and to guide your reading. Factory representatives, people in associations, and professionals may provide you with the kind of early direction you need as a writing detective. Covering some leads on the phone and others in person; listing and asking questions; and taking and transcribing good notes—all constitute the first big steps in hunting.

What do you get when you talk to an expert, whether your predecessor or a professor of computer technology? You get information, both oral and written. For example, your expert may hand you a magazine article or two, even a book, that contains the exact information you want. In other words, the person you've interviewed has already done some research for you—free of charge. You may, in fact, find all the answers you need in your first interview. But even if you don't, you should have more leads.

How do you question an expert? The best way is to state your interest and then begin with an open-ended question. For example: "I'm writing a proposal for new word-processing and database applications for our corporate training office. Do you have any ideas or suggestions on the kind of equipment or requirements I should look for?" This kind of a wide-open question should induce any expert to wax eloquently, which in turn will lead you to other questions. By starting with broad questions, you'll stimulate a relaxed and free-flowing dialogue. From there you'll find the interviewing process a natural one.

Before you get right into questioning your experts, however, you must establish a degree of rapport with them—you have to earn the right to ask them a question. This is a ritual of all societies. If you walk up to a total stranger on your commuter train and begin asking a series of questions about anything but the time, your chances of meeting with resistance are high. However, if you strike up a friendly, low-key discussion about the commute, you can then gradually discuss where you work and what you do. Eventually your commuting acquaintance may allow you to ask more probing questions.

The same holds true when you talk to experts. Introduce yourself and tell them what you want to do. If you expect their help, you must first give them information. Tell them why you came to them, and they'll start off flattered. If you believe that these people know their stuff, tell them so. You'll immediately score points and open the door to discussion.

One interview may lead to several others, and in little time you can focus on a particular idea. Turning this idea into words early on makes hunting and subsequent writing much easier.

DEVELOPING A THESIS STATEMENT

Purpose gives direction to your work and life. If you decide to run in marathons, you'll immediately begin to run progressively more miles, sleep properly, eat well, and perhaps read running magazines. Your decision to run in marathons gives you direction. In writing it is the same. You must develop a central focus, or thesis as it's called in writing, to set you on your hunting path.

Let's say your initial idea was simply computers. Without focus, your hunt would involve the interviewing of thousands of people and the reading of hundreds, maybe even thousands, of books and periodicals. Who knows if you'd ever get anywhere. Even "computers at work," though still a very rough idea, would considerably narrow your focus. In hunting for your thesis, you'd no longer need to worry about video games or home applications—you'd eliminate much of your research.

If you can refine your search to a single focus, which you hope to support with your writing, you'll have developed a thesis statement and will be well on the way to successful hunting. You might try as a potential thesis statement: "Certain microcomputer applications in the training office would make the office more effective and efficient." Can you see how this statement makes your purpose more direct and clear than the initial one of computers? You've merely narrowed the focus.

To refine your ideas and develop your thesis statement you should ask yourself: "What am I trying to do (or to prove) in this paper?" If you find it difficult to write a developed thesis, try talking it out with someone—rehearse your purpose. Indeed, some people come to writing through oral communication. As you explain your paper to a friend or spouse, you'll begin to connect your ideas, which will help you put them into a single provable statement: your thesis statement.

Does this mean that you can't change this newly developed thesis statement? No. You'll revise this one as you learn new information, but eventually, you will find a statement that exactly suits our purpose. Also, when you begin hunting, don't worry if you're not sure what you're looking for. Most writers start off blindly, discovering their path as they go. So, you can begin interviewing with only a minithesis in mind. The sooner you develop your specific point of focus, however, the more efficiently you will be able to interview, and the faster your writing will go.

WHERE TO FIND SOURCES

Once you've talked with the people who can help you in your quest, turn to institutions. You will find sources located in companies, associations, and libraries.

Never, for example, neglect the institutional knowledge you can find stored away in company files. Depending on the extent and comprehensiveness of your organization's filing systems, you may find all the information you need tucked safely away in company files. Why not check what the institution already has to offer?

Second, consider associations. Associations in Washington, D.C., the origin of many associations, number in the thousands, for everything from car dealers to concrete manufacturers. Associations can store vast amounts of specialized industry-related data. For example, the National Association of Broadcasters houses a fine library, chock full of data on the industry—a necessary stop for anyone writing a paper on the media.

Third, and most familiar to most of us, is the institution called the library. Eventually, we all end up in the library. It is an invaluable resource. Neither this chapter nor this book will turn you into a research expert, but both seek to introduce you to various resources and the research process. You should locate several places and people in your library: the card catalogue, the reader's guides to periodical literature, and the research librarians.

The card catalogue lists the library's collection of books in three ways: by title, by author, and by subject. Thus, *The Computer in Business* by John Doe could be found either under *Computer in Business, The* (its title); Doe, John (its author); or computer business (its subject). Quickly leafing through the subject catalogue, which is automated in many libraries, will give you a good general idea of what your library has available in your topic area. Often you can establish your bedrock research with this stop in the library.

Since the cycle of book publication often takes two years, you'll have to turn to periodicals and newspapers for current information. Most libraries have a periodical room for you to find out the most up-to-date information. Here you'll discover a myriad of indexes: *The Social Science Index, The Business Index, The Criminal Justice Periodical Index, The*

Reader's Guide to Periodical Literature, and an array of others, including newspaper indexes (*The New York Times, The Washington Post*, etc.). Indeed, libraries now have many of these indexes on computer, giving you direct access to them with the touch of a keyboard. Though each index presents its information differently, all are arranged, at the least, by topic. Thus, by searching appropriate indexes you can usually substantially update your research.

   Finally, never overlook the librarians, especially the research librarians. They can help you find almost anything, while introducing you to resources you've never imagined. If you expect to research and write on a regular basis, be sure to establish a friendly working relationship with the research librarians at the outset. You will earn their respect early on by doing your homework before talking to them. That is, before you ask a question, make sure you've already tried to solve the problem yourself. Always tell the librarians that you've checked this, that, and then this other thing—all to no avail. They will then know you're not using them as a card catalogue and usually will go out of their way to help a fellow researcher. By doing your homework, you automatically build a bond of respect and trust with librarians.

INTERVIEWING BOOKS

Most of us interview other people simply by talking with them. We do it everyday—at work, at home, and in social settings. Gleaning information from others is nothing new. "How are you?" "What's new?" "How many days will it take to deliver?" But when it comes to "interviewing" books or printed resources, people tend to balk, and they shouldn't.

A book, for example, is pretty much mute, until you know how to get it talking. Start by asking it a few easy questions.

First, just by looking at the title page you can find out a lot about what's inside: at the very least, the title, the author, the place of publication, and the publisher.

Second, the book itself provides at least one—and often two—excellent finder mechanisms: the table of contents and the index. Skim the table of contents first to see if the book covers your area of interest and also to see if you may have overlooked any related items. Next, scan the index in the back of the book. Most lengthy manuscripts include indexes that help you quickly locate specific subtopical areas, and your quick perusal can pay big dividends by telling you whether you want to check out the book or put it back in the stacks.

Once you've decided that you want to use a book or periodical, you've got to record your "interview." Many people have a hard time developing a systematic method to record information and research. Why not consider what many professional writers do: recording their sources, and using notecards, notesheets, or photocopies. First, we'll look at making bibliography cards, then at making notecards.

Bibliography Cards

You need a system to record both the books and periodicals you've used and the people you've interviewed so you can readily refer back to them. Use either a notecard or a notesheet to record the pertinent data: title, author, date and place of publication, edition number, publisher, and page numbers if it's a periodical. Also, for your own help, record the book's call sign and the library you found it in, especially if you plan to use several libraries. Alternatively, you can photocopy the title page, along with the table of contents, index, or both. This method is much quicker and often more comprehensive.

Next, number each bibliography card or page consecutively (that is, label the first book you reviewed number one, and so on). Thus, each resource will have a unique identifier for you to use when you begin taking notes. Remember to keep your bibliography cards or sheets separate from your notes so you can control your data.

Notecards and Notesheets

Collecting information from books, periodicals, and even interviews requires an orderly system. Disorder early in the research process leads to late confusion and dismay in your writing. You can avoid frustration by employing a simple, time-tested system of information handling: the systematic use of notecards or notesheets. Specifically, you should produce a notecard or notesheet for every piece of information or idea you find worthy of recording. This section will explain how to use a slug line, how to paraphrase (and why you should), and what other information to include on the card.

First, create a slug line. When you record information on any notecard, always summarize the contents of your source in a single, short synopsis sentence, just like a headline. For example: "Computers save work, money, and time." Put this slug on the top of a card, *then* go on to explore the views of your expert on these areas. The slug line gives you a quick reference and synopsis so that weeks or months later when you are ready to write, you can sort your cards without having to read the entire entry. Slug lines are great time-savers.

Second, when possible, paraphrase the information you collect. Long, involved quotes strung together in a paper look like artificial fillers, the product of a writer too lazy to assimilate and interpret the data. Further, and even more disturbing, the patchwork of multiple styles that results from too many direct quotes has a Frankenstein effect on your writing: your writing won't be *your* writing at all.

On the other hand, when you paraphrase, you learn and assimilate knowledge—a major purpose of writing. Further, your writing rings true: it sounds like you wrote it, not someone else. With only one owner, your writing also carries an even, clear tone—something readers really appreciate. Remember, if you do have to quote someone—because the language is so good or the corroboration from a noteworthy source so pertinent—make the quotes short and sweet. Avoid long block quotes.

Third, always record specific locator information on each card. Remember to include the number you have assigned on the information's bibliography card. Many people put this number in a circle in the upper righthand corner of all the cards. Next, write the slug line at the top of the card, and underline it for emphasis. And make sure you include the source's page number for future reference and footnoting purposes. Once you've completed the notecard, file it away. Before long, you'll begin to see patterns developing in your notes that later will become useful when you prepare to write.

SYSTEMATIC PROCESS

Hunting is a miniprocess within the writing process itself. First, you begin with what you know—your writing draft. Next, you interview people who know the subject—experienced others and experts. Through open-ended questions, they can provide you with productive leads to follow up that can save you enormous amounts of time. With information in hand, develop your thesis—the statement you propose to prove in your writing. Your thesis will be a guiding light for you and the reader. With thesis in hand, head for institutions like companies, associations, and libraries to find more sources of information.

Use notecards or notesheets to record information. Don't forget the critical identification information on each card, and pay attention to accuracy and detail. By having a systematic method to take notes from your sources, you will make your research a much more manageable process.

Using these steps in the hunting process will make your work more systematic and, in the end, easier.

PROCESSWRITING WORKSHOP
HUNTING #5

Now that you've completed your survey, you're ready to begin filling in the holes—the gaps you may have found in your writing. To make the job of filling those holes more efficient, you can take several steps in a process called hunting.

Objectives

1. To record relevant information from resources.
2. To collect sufficient information to write the paper.

Activities

Step 1
Interview people who know about your topic. Find an expert or two and get some leads before you go to the library.

Step 2
Review your notes and interviews, and try to write one sentence that focuses your thoughts on the topic—your thesis. To help, finish this sentence: In this paper I will prove that _____. A thesis sentence tells you and the reader what you'll support with your research and writing.

Step 3

With your thesis statement and some leads in mind, go to company files and documents and to the library (corporate, public, etc.). Use the card catalogue, the magazine guides, any available databases, and government documents to formulate a working bibliography. Like the working outline, this bibliography represents your best guess at references that might work well for your project. This tentative list will be subject to additions and deletions, so keep an open mind.

Step 4

Begin taking notes. Develop a slug line for each card that matches your working outline. Paraphrase the source in your own words. If a new but important topic appears, add a new line to the outline. Next, add bibliographic reference and page number.

Illustration

Step 1: Interviewing Experts

I chose to interview our computer expert, Mary Jane Byte. She explained to me that we already had a file in our company records about the application of computers to training. Further, she indicated that I should look at the brochures that she has on Company XYZ because they contain an example relevant to my project. Finally, she referred me to an *ORD Computer* magazine article dated January 1987, entitled "Modernizing the Training Process," by Blume and Sollie. She also agreed to look over my draft later to make sure I didn't misinterpret anything. The interview took twenty minutes and headed me in the right direction.

Step 2: Writing a Thesis Sentence

In this memo I will prove that computers can improve my training operation.

Step 3: Developing a Working Bibliography

Source 1: Interview with Mary Jane Byte, company computer coordinator, conducted January 17, 1987.

Source 2: Article entitled "Modernizing the Training Process," by Blume and Sollie, in *ORD Computer* magazine, dated January 1987.

Source 3: Company file entitled, "Computer Applications," file # Computer-143514.

Step 4: Taking Notes

Bibliography Cards

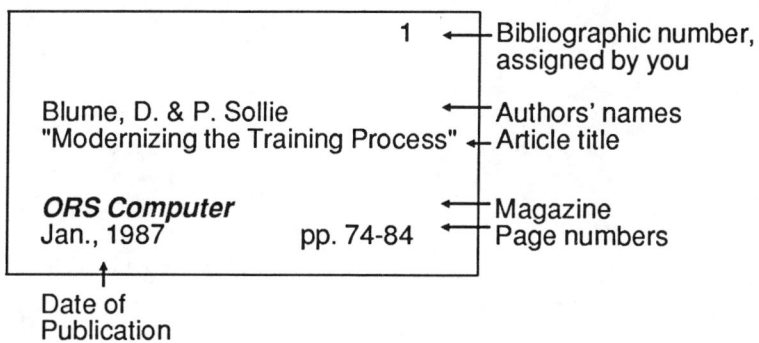

Note Cards

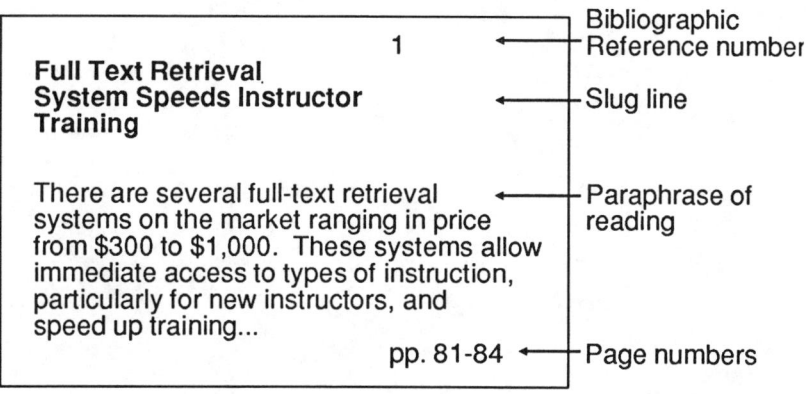

6. WRITING

Early in the writing process you did some writing, remember? You freewrote or freespoke—used one of the fastwriting techniques that helped you get your ideas on paper quickly—to find out what you knew about your topic. Well, now you're going to do it all over again, only this time with the benefit of some notes—what you learned from others about the topic. This step of the writing process integrates what you know already with the information you've learned while hunting. In this chapter you'll learn how to organize your notes, how to use your preliminary outline, how to refine your thesis, and how to write freely with new information.

ORGANIZING YOUR NOTES

In the hunting step you tested the water of opinion and knowledge: you found out what others had to say about your topic. No doubt you've accumulated a pile of notecards or notesheets for your efforts. So now what? Well, now you need to sort out the information so you can use it wisely in a draft.

Begin by reading each of your slug lines and placing each card in a specific pile. Remember that key word list you made, that tentative outline of ideas? Now is a good time to retrieve that list and review each word for its potential as an outline heading. Use this list to create the categories for your card piles. When you reach a card that doesn't fit into any existing categories, add a new one to your list. You're starting to flesh out the outline. Now you're ready for the next step.

Thoroughly reread each of the cards in the particular categories. After that, read them again. Most people require three to four readings to master the information, and that's what the writing step is all about: the mastery and assimilation of information.

As already mentioned, when you read each card and check it against your rough, key word outline, you'll find yourself revising the outline by adding and deleting key words. Remember, outlines are always evolving: as you learn more, you refine them more.

At this point, after you have reviewed your notes extensively, a few things will occur. First, you'll realize that you've collected some irrelevant information. Invariably, as you cast a wide net to catch information, you find that you'll take in more fish than you'll ever need. So, throw them back. Just put the notes in a file and save them, or use them to start a new fire next winter. You may toss out as much as 50 percent of your notes. Remember, the purpose of research is to determine what's out there and then collect it. When you begin a quest, you're not at all sure what you'll need, so you collect everything. But once you begin paring it down, you should look critically at what you can and cannot use.

Next, you'll note that your rough, key word outline needs finer tuning—one of the purposes of the writing step. New words and ideas will begin finding their way into your writing. You'll go back and forth from your notes to your working outline, and soon you'll arrive at a very rough outline or map of your paper. You don't need to have a full-formed plan to write your draft. However, some people prefer to produce an exact outline during this step. We will examine the form for a final outline in the next chapter, so, for now, let's assume you will stick to your working outline.

Now, with assimilated notes in hand, you've got an outline that gives a general direction to your upcoming draft. But before you begin, you need a still clearer vision of where you're going. The best way to get that is to develop a more concise thesis statement.

REFINING THE THESIS STATEMENT

Remember when you developed a rough thesis statement to help your hunting? Now it's time to refine that statement, if you haven't already done so. Having thoroughly read all of your notecards, you should be in a good position to refine your statement based on the additional information.

First, read your notes once more. Then, sit back and pretend you're talking to a friend. The friend should be an "intelligent ignorant": a well-read, interested, and ready listener who happens to know little about your topic. You may even find it useful to make a tape recording of your imaginary conversation. Tell her or him what your paper is all about. Try to reduce the topic to a single thesis sentence—the point you want to support with all the evidence you've collected.

Why is a thesis so important? Because it directs and limits what you include in your paper. If, for example, your thesis reads "Computers in training offices require a wide range of software," your development of that thesis will be much different from one that states, "Computers in training save teachers time and increase their productivity." Both of these theses revolve around computers in training, yet they will produce two very different papers. Notice that when you develop a clear thesis, you make writing a draft a much simpler task.

WRITING THE DRAFT

Now comes the fun part: writing. You need only refer to chapter 4 for the techniques. To produce a draft, use one of the scrawling, fastwriting techniques: freewriting, freelisting, webbing, or freespeaking. To create a full-text draft immediately, you should use either freewriting or freespeaking. You must eventually convert the other two systems to a text; thus, they add another step to your process.

When you freewrite or freespeak be careful to keep going, even if your words still need polishing. Keep pushing forward and, if possible, avoid reading your cards. Of course, you can refer to the notes to give your draft a fresh and natural tone, but try to do this sparingly.

Also, try to produce this working draft as quickly as you can, with as few interruptions as possible. Keep the flow going; get the draft out so you'll have something to work with. Once you've completed the draft, put it down for a day or two to get some distance from it. Remember, time can work for you as long as you don't allow it to turn into procrastination. Time lets you review the draft with fresh eyes.

REVIEWING THE DRAFT

When you read through your draft, you will find some holes. Some of the holes you'll be able to fill immediately, and some you won't.

First, you'll find information you left out, because you forgot it or had trouble explaining it. Perhaps, for example, you were writing your draft on computerizing the training office, and when you got to computerizing lesson plans you got a phone call and lost your train of thought. Now, with a clear mind, you should be able to spot this gaping hole and plug it in immediately.

Second, holes can and do occur, not just because of oversight, but because of underthought as well. In such cases you will have to review your notes and sometimes return to the library or a specific source for more information. Or you simply may have to take more time rereading your notes to assimilate the information you've already collected.

This step in the writing process produces the first draft. Now you have something you can mold—add to and take away from. You've taken a big step toward completing your writing by producing this draft, and you'll be amazed at how fast you will complete the remaining steps.

PROCESSWRITING WORKSHOP
WRITING #6

Now that you've done some research and have gotten some hard facts, you're ready to write a first draft of your paper. How do you start? It's easy. Just go back to your favorite fastwriting style.

Objectives
1. To organize and sort resource cards.
2. To develop a consistent voice throughout the paper.

Activities
Step 1
Review all of your notecards and match them to your working outline. Revise the outline where necessary. Share your outline with your writing process partner for feedback.

Step 2
After reviewing your notes, refine your thesis statement. Talk to a hypothetical "intelligent ignorant," explaining in one sentence what you hope to develop in your paper.

Step 3

Review your cards again and set aside any that don't fit your thesis. Don't throw them away because you might change your mind later.

Step 4

Study your notes intensely. Describe the substance of your report to your partner.

Step 5

Now you are ready to write your first draft. Put your notes away. As fast as you can, freespeak or freewrite, based on what you remember from the notes and your own common knowledge. Take twenty minutes for this exercise. Again, don't worry about spelling or mechanics, just let the words fly.

Illustration
Step 1: Revising the Outline

After reviewing my notecards, I made the following revision to my initial working outline. I added *quick-find* system, a system that allows full text retrieval; *full check*, a program that checks the spelling of word processing; *hard disk*, for increased storage; and *screen covers*, which reduce screen glare for users.

> Training
> Lesson plans
> Word processing
> Database
> Communication skills
> Productivity
> Scheduling system
> ABC Computer Company
> XYZ Computer Company
> Performance
> Storage
> Retrieval
> Costs
> Quick-find
> Full check
> Hard disk
> Screen covers

Step 2: Refining the Thesis Statement

In this memo I will prove that the effectiveness and efficiency of communications training can be significantly improved through the use of computers.

Step 3: Reviewing the Notecards

I went through my cards and found out that I had to toss out about 30 percent of the cards that I had gathered. I had gathered about 10 cards, and I put three aside.

Step 4: Studying the Notes

I spend about twenty to thirty minutes reviewing my cards before entering step 5.

Step 5: Freewriting the First Draft

Teaching communications to executives of a multinational ping-pong ball manufacturing company is my job. In delivering communication packages to executive groups, it is clear to me that we need to become more effective and efficient.

With respect to word processing, it was recommended by M. J. Byte in a personal interview that we develop a series of lesson plans written on hard disks as well as stored on soft disks to enhance the effectiveness of our operation. I surveyed the turnover in our Training Office for the past six years and found that there have been a total of six instructors who have come and gone—each one having to learn about the lesson plans by word of mouth. According to Byte, having all these plans on file would allow new instructors to pull the lesson plans "off the shelf" when necessary and have at their fingertips the historical memory of the office. This, rather than relying on the institutional memory of those few who remain in this highly mobile office, would allow incoming instructors to come up to speed more quickly, thus improving their efficiency. The word processor will also eliminate the need for the extra secretarial or typing help that is being considered at this time. A new secretary would cost approximately $28,000 per year, a typist $22,000, and the total software and hardware for this program is estimated to be a total of $65,000, and thus would be paid for in less than three years based on secretarial costs alone. Two real problems in the office are not having some form of an indexing and not having a retrieval system for lesson plans. Through research in *ORD Computer* magazine, I discovered a system that is now available for $700 called "Quick-Find." Quick-Find allows full text retrieval in an indexing system that will give ready access to any disk data. So whenever anyone new comes into the office, he or she will be able, with a series of commands, to pull up any information he or she needs based on indexing commands. For example, if instructors want to know what is on file on nonverbal communications, they can enter the words **nonverbal communication** on the command line, and all the information will be pulled up from the stored lesson plans. A computer can also serve as a scheduler for the office. My office requires an enormous amount of scheduling because our training takes place on demand and at both on-site and off-site locations. According to *Computer*

Match magazine, "Schedule Master" ($600)—a software package that is available—can meet our company's needs. This program will be able to track all of our appointments and schedules as well as all of our communications that are incoming and outgoing, so that we can track when we send information out on our processors.

Regarding microcomputers, I've looked specifically at ABC computers and XYZ computers and found that because the ABC computers are the most widespread in industry and have the greatest amount of business software, that even though they are more expensive ($1,000 more expensive), their likely suitability over the long run seems to be far greater than any other. I estimate we will need four terminals: one for secretarial/typing support, two on remote-independent stations for instructors' use, and one at my desk for management control. The estimated cost for hardware is $60,000-plus.

7. REVISING

You've finally gotten your ideas and research down in writing. Sure, your draft isn't the prettiest piece of polished writing you've ever seen, but remember, you've conquered the toughest part: getting your topic on paper. The next few steps go quickly because you can work with a concrete piece of writing.

Now it's time to take the writing that makes sense to you and fashion it to make sense to others: your readers. The revising step marks a shift in your writing process. You shift your concern from producing your ideas to communicating those ideas to others. In a sense, you shift from being author-centered to being reader-centered.

In this chapter you'll look at how to make your writing explicable to readers through well-constructed paragraphs. You will learn to scan your draft for related ideas, develop topic sentences, create unity with transitions, and watch paragraph length. In short, you'll learn how to write effective paragraphs.

SCANNING THE DRAFT

The first revising activity for writing effective paragraphs is to scan your entire draft quickly and look for related ideas. You'll find that in early freewriting you scatter your ideas more than in the latter stages of writing. This phenomenon is easily explained.

In the beginning, your mind has trouble focusing; thus, your thoughts start, stop, and shift. But once you get started, your thinking, and consequently your writing, seem to settle down into more logical grooves. Some English professors tell their students to tear off the first page of their papers before turning in the remaining pages to them. These instructors have discovered that unnecessary writing generally fills that first page, so they see little sense in reading it.

So, review your draft. Using a lettering system of A, B, C, D or a numbering system of 1, 2, 3, 4, 5 will help you label similar ideas in your draft. Remember to put apples with apples and oranges with oranges. This first revising step is macroscopic: you want to get an overall logical grouping of ideas.

Now that you've labeled like ideas, move them closer to each other. If you use a colored pencil, simply draw arrows. If the movement requires a major shift, you might do well to arrange sheets of paper or notecards, just as you did when hunting. Sheets or cards are simple but effective organizing tools of the trade. By listing the related ideas on a single document, you'll be able to concentrate on the related ideas as a whole.

Having done that, you're ready for a second organizing principle: the topic sentence.

DEVELOPING TOPIC SENTENCES

When you review each of your idea groupings—particularly if you've put nearly identical ideas together—you'll see patterns develop. For example, if you're writing about computers in the work setting, you may find a group of sentences dealing with the efficiency of computers: "Computers allow quick revisions requiring little effort." "Computers store enormous amounts of data in small amounts of space." "Computers permit even the novice typist to produce near-perfect drafts through revision." When you step back from these related statements, you can see a pattern evolving: they all deal with computer efficiency. Now, write a single sentence to encapsulate the general theme of this group of sentences. You might write: "Computers are efficient in a work setting." By writing this overview statement, you've just written a topic sentence for a paragraph. Easy enough?

Where should you place the topic sentence in a paragraph? Theoretically, you can put it anywhere. Realistically, you should write it at the beginning of the paragraph to provide a forecast of coming events. What else does the topic sentence do for your readers? It gives them a conceptual overview of what follows: it offers a preview of coming attractions. The topic sentence tells the reader what to expect and, at the same time, hints at the facts that follow. For example:

> It takes very few seconds to perform this function. It is a multistepped operation that necessitates dexterity. The individual with keen motor development can accomplish it with relative ease, and the results are startling, immediate, and rewarding. Most of all, it's a healthy, cheap, and simple way to ensure a relatively germ-free society.

What's this paragraph about? Without a topic sentence up front to give you an overview, you find it difficult, if not impossible, to understand it. This paragraph's topic sentence might well be: "Washing your hands is a step-by-step process that can prevent germs." Now reread the paragraph, and undoubtedly it will make more sense to you. Why? Because you had some idea about its objective before you got the details. So now you know how the topic sentence operates. We learn particulars more easily when they follow a general overview.

Think about how difficult you find it when a child or a friend runs up to you and gives you a series of facts with no reference: "It's bleeding, the street's a mess, John's crying, it's not my fault." Though you may be able to piece this one together, you usually have to ask, "What's this all about?" Then you get a topic sentence like "John fell off his bike." Now the facts (bleeding, crying, etc.) make sense, because you can fit them into an overall framework.

Again, to develop a topic sentence (1) review your related sentences and (2) write out a sentence that summarizes them. Remember, the sentences following your topic sentence should support and prove it. They must relate directly back to the topic sentence. Keep apples with apples—don't mix. If in one paragraph you talk about a computer's efficiency in the worksetting, don't wander off into its recreational uses. Save that for another paragraph, maybe even another chapter.

MAKING TRANSITIONS

Just as topic sentences *unify* the whole paragraph (give overall meaning to its facts), transition sentences *organize* the pieces of writing within the paragraph. Thus, writing can be unified but disorganized. Even as they travel down a well-developed topic sentence, the readers need some road signs—transitions—to your writing. Devices such as conjunctions, pronouns, repeated words, and synonyms provide these road signs. In this section you'll learn how transitions can help your writing and your readers.

The role of a writer is much like that of a tour guide. Your readers trail right behind you: all look to see what you point out, and all follow you with at least moderate attention. However, if you give a false direction, or no direction at all, you'll miscue your pack of interested followers and sometimes even lose them.

Conjunctions are just one way of keeping readers on track. You may know where you're going, but your readers won't unless you give them a hint. So, words such as *and, but, as, as well as, also, however, therefore, thus, further,* and *moreover*, as well as directive phrases such as *in contrast, on the other hand*, and *in other words*, all depict the relationship of one part of your writing to another.

To illustrate, if you write, "Computers are useful in the office setting, but...," the reader has a clue from the word **but** that what follows will oppose or contrast what you've just said. On the other hand (see how this phrase will work on you as a reader), if you were to say, "Computers are useful in the office setting, therefore...," your reader expects you to draw a conclusion, because words like **thus** and **therefore** imply a conclusion. Thus (see, there it is again!), by using specific transitional words you can cue your readers and keep them on track. Remember, transitions help readers understand relationships. The following list will help you with transitions:

Relationship	**Transition**
addition	also, and, moreover, further, similarly, likewise
comparison	in the same way, likewise
opposition/contrast	but, however, on the other hand, yet
example	for example, for instance
cause and effect	as a result, thus, therefore, hence

Relationship	Transition
time and/or space	above, around, earlier, soon, then
summary	at last, finally, in conclusion, in summary

Transitions serve as the signposts that help readers stay with you. If you shift directions, give them a hint—an inclination of your new direction. They'll appreciate your help and reward you by reading on instead of discarding your writing for something less frustrating.

PRONOUNS

One simple method of offering transitions in your writing is to use pronouns. Pronouns are stand-ins (they substitute for nouns) that refer back to your subject: thus, they provide a link—a transition. If you say, "Computer research indicates high usage in the daytime. It also indicates...," the reader knows that *it* refers back to *computer research.* You've provided transition without any boring repetition. However, use caution with your pronouns. Make sure they enhance clarity rather than confuse your meaning. For example: "The men and women stopped by the gym, and then they stopped to put on makeup." Obviously, you didn't mean that the men put on makeup. So, watch how, when, and where you place pronouns. Keep them close to their nouns, and if any possibility of confusion exists, restate the noun or start a new sentence: "The men and women stopped by the gym, and then the women stopped to put on makeup." Or, "The men and women stopped by the gym. The women then stopped to put on their makeup."

REPEATED WORDS AND SYNONYMS

As a final method of transition in your paragraphs, try either repeating a word from one sentence to another or using a synonym. Both of these techniques keep the flow of the paragraph going.

To illustrate, read the following:

> The company's president entered the room and sat down at the conference table to begin the meeting. We had called the meeting to discuss the purchase of several new products that would increase the efficiency of the office. We scheduled all such conferences in the morning because the boss was happiest then.

Notice how the writer used *meeting* in the first sentence and then repeated it in the next to keep up the flow. But in sentence three, the writer substituted *conference* for *meeting*. Also, see how the synonym *boss* in the last sentence gets us back to the *company's president* in a way that fits the tone of the sentence. The paragraph flows because of the transitional elements, repetition, and use of synonyms.

PARAGRAPH LENGTH

How long should you make your paragraphs? Some might say, "As long as they need to be." But such an answer, while theoretically correct, gives little practical help to the people asking the question. As a general guide, try to keep your sentence length to two or three typed lines. Make paragraphs three to five sentences long—about 75 to 125 words.

In easy-to-remember terms, when you look at a double-spaced typed page, it ought to have at least two paragraphs per page. Why? Because paragraphs are meant to focus on *one* thought, not several. Second, they are intended to be breaks or resting stops for readers. When paragraphs get too long or involved, they violate both of these intentions. Long, involved paragraphs become tedious and confusing to readers, breaking their concentration and losing interest.

COMMUNICATING YOUR IDEAS

Paragraphs are designed for readers, not writers. They encourage a reader's understanding and come at a time in the writing process when you, as a writer, must shift from idea production—getting your ideas down on paper—to idea communication. You must direct that communication to your readers.

Readers need your help. Remember, *you* know what you're saying, but your readers do not. Help them by developing sound, well-written paragraphs. Use clearly designed topic sentences, and weave transitional elements into each paragraph so readers can easily follow the development of your ideas. If communication is the objective of writing, understanding is paramount, and paragraph development essential.

PROCESSWRITING WORKSHOP
REVISING #7

With the first draft you have produced ideas that are invaluable to your writing. But those ideas often are jumbled and unrefined—raw material. The initial editing process, revising, helps you put apples with apples. It helps you order your ideas into coherent paragraphs for future, more refined drafts.

Objectives

1. To organize ideas.
2. To develop internal unity within paragraphs.

Activities

Step 1

Go through your writing draft quickly and group similar ideas. Label these ideas with A, B, C, etc.; 1, 2, 3, etc.; or with color codes from colored pencils. Any device will do, so long as it groups similar ideas. Remember, don't put apples with oranges: apples go with other apples and oranges with other oranges.

Step 2

Now group the ideas into paragraphs of three to seven sentences. Longer or shorter ones can cause comprehension difficulties for the reader. Look at your grouped sentences and come up with one sentence that sums up the paragraph. This sentence, your topic sentence, will introduce the paragraph by giving the reader an overview of what follows.

Step 3

Look for ways to link the paragraphs so they flow naturally from one to another—a technique called transition. Repeat one of the last words of one paragraph in the topic sentence of the next. Use pronouns that refer back to a previous sentence or use connectives like *and, but, however, also, further,* and *moreover.*

Illustration
Step 1: Regrouping Ideas
NOTE: I've labeled, grouped and initially paragraphed my draft from chapter 6. It's still rough, but like ideas are together and are easier to work with.

Teaching communications to executives of a multi-national ping-pong ball manufacturing company is my job. In delivering communication packages to executive groups, it is clear to me that we need to become more effective and efficient.

With respect to [A]*word processing*, it was recommended by M. J. Byte in a personal interview that we develop a series of lesson plans written on hard disks as well as stored on soft disks to enhance the effectiveness of our operation. I surveyed the turnover in our Training Office for the past six years and found that there have been a total of six different instructors who have come and gone, each one having to learn about the lesson plans by word of mouth. According to Byte, having all these plans on file would allow new instructors to pull the lesson plans "off the shelf" when necessary and have at their fingertips the historical memory of the office. This, rather than relying on the institutional memory of those few who remain in this highly mobile office, would allow incoming instructors to come up to speed more quickly, thus improving their efficiency.

A new secretary would cost approximately $28,000 per year, a typist $22,000, and the total software and hardware for this program is estimated to be a total of $65,000, and thus would be paid for in less than three years based on secretarial costs alone.

New instructors need access to lesson plans on file for efficiency. Our old word-of-mouth system is not effective. In the office we don't have any form of an ^{B}*indexing*/retrieval system for lesson plans.

There is inexpensive indexing/retrieval software that will help new instructors. Through research in *ORS Computer* magazine, I discovered a system that is now available for $700 called "Quick-Find." Quick-Find allows full-text retrieval in an ^{B}*indexing system* that will give ready access to any disk data. So whenever anyone new comes into the office, he or she will be able, with a series of commands, to pull up any information he or she needs based on ^{B}*indexing* commands. For example, if instructors want to know what is on file on nonverbal communications, they can enter the words **nonverbal communication** on the command line, and all the information will be pulled up from the stored lesson plans.

A computer can serve as a ^{C}*scheduler* for the office. My office requires an enormous amount of scheduling because our training takes place on demand and at both on-site and off-site locations. According to *Computer Match* magazine, "Schedule Master" ($600)—a software package that is available—can meet our company's needs. This program will be able to track all of our appointments and ^C*schedules* as well as all of our communications that are incoming and outgoing so that we can track when we send information out on our processors.

Regarding ^D*microcomputers*, I've looked specifically at ^D*ABC computers and XYZ computers* and found that because the ABC computers are the most widespread in industry and have the greatest amount of business software, that even though they are more expensive ($1,000 more expensive), their likely suitability over the long run seems to be far greater than any other. I estimate we will need four ^D*terminals:* one for secretarial/ typing support, two on remote-independent stations for instructors' use, and one at my desk for management control. The estimated cost for hardware is $60,000-plus.

Step 2: Writing the Topic Sentence

We currently have a turnover problem in the Training Office caused by not enough secretarial support. All instructors are required to produce lesson plans for each one of their classes. Presently, with six instructors in the office, one secretary, and very limited typing support, the instructors are forced either to type on their own or to use handwritten notes that only they can read. This causes problems, such as loss of instructional memory when instructors leave. And over the last six years, six instructors have left, taking their lesson plans with them. According to Byte, having lesson plans on a word-processing disk file would allow new instructors to pull their lesson plans "off the shelf," thus preserving the historical/institutional memory of the office.

Step 3: Link the Paragraphs

Word processing can *also* (transition word) save money in the long run. Presently, we are considering hiring an additional secretary or clerk-typist, which would cost in excess of $22,000 per year. The total estimate for computer software (programs) and hardware would be approximately $65,000, which would amortize typing costs in only three years.

8. REWRITING

REWRITING

Buildings, automobiles, and virtually all objects have some type of structure to give them form. Written documents are no different. Certain structural conventions, if followed, give any document the form it needs to stand on its own.

Any well-constructed document contains three major structural elements: the introduction, the body, and the conclusion. This chapter will explore all three elements in detail, as well as show how they compose the overall structure of any organized piece of writing.

Regardless of what you write, this format—introduction, body, conclusion—provides a basic structure. For example, memoranda, though very short, contain an introduction—usually the reference or purpose line—which states the thesis of the memorandum. This thesis—the controlling topical sentence—gives the reader the direction and scope of the memorandum. Longer memorandum reports, those of several pages, are also commonly found in business and government. These reports usually contain a summary or executive summary paragraph right in the beginning before providing any details. Longer reports, ranging from twenty to fifty pages, have an introductory section that, among other things, explains specialized vocabulary used in the report. Further, they feature an abstract of the key topical sentences of the document, in addition to the index. For book-length documents, an introductory chapter is appropriate. Such a chapter provides topical and structural guidance to the reader. Thus, the longer the document, the more structure it needs to help the reader.

Structure is intended for readers, not for writers. Writers understand what they write about, but structure helps convey these ideas to readers. All structure seems to have this general format: the introduction, the body, and the conclusion. You should allow 15 percent of the total document length for the introduction, 75 percent for the body, and 10 percent for the conclusion.

THE INTRODUCTION

Let's begin with the introduction. First, you need to get your reader's attention. Generally, you compete with many others—though not necessarily all writers—for a reader's time. So, when creating a document, whether a memo, report, or whatever, try to begin with a startling statistic or idea that will draw attention to your topic. A statistic that makes the reader say, "Wow, I didn't know this!" works particularly well. A second method might begin with several rhetorical questions. One question can be effective; two or three seem to have more impact on the reader; more than three questions becomes tedious. Third, you might begin with some sort of a short story, something brief and illustrative. Finally, you might pose a hypothetical situation that will engage the reader's interest.

Attention-getters can be very brief or extended, depending on the type of business document. Longer documents, ones requiring a definite commitment of time by the audience, need more of an attention-getter than shorter memorandum-type documents.

The second area in the introduction establishes the paper's importance to the readers. They need to know why they should read this document. What's special about it? Why should they care about it? In short: What can you (the writer) do for them (the readers)? The more routine, responsive, and informative your writing, the less you need to establish a "need to know" in the reader. In fact, this step is often left out in short, routine, and straightforward memos.

However, the more persuasive your aim, the more you must establish the problem and the need in the reader. Consider, for example, how television affects the daily lives of your readers. As parents and consumers, your readers need to be sensitive to television. Thus, establishing this need in the introduction rivets their attention and gets your writing read.

The third part of a good introduction establishes the thesis of the paper. The thesis, which is generally cast as a declarative sentence, sets forth the writer's perspective on a topic. Presented early in the document, the thesis should set the tone and focus—the direction—of the paper for both reader and writer.

Let's look at an example. You might choose the topic of television viewing. One thesis sentence for this subject might be: "Television viewing, while educational in certain circumstances, often incites violent activity in children."

This particular thesis sentence signifies that you will say something specific about the impact of television and indicates the kind of language you might use in your paper. Right at the start, it gives your readers an idea of the reservations you have about television viewing. In short, the thesis tells the readers something about where your paper is going, and what they can expect.

Usually you get to the thesis by asking yourself questions that continually seek the focus of your particular topic. This process may require a bull's-eye approach. Start with a word in an outer ring. Divide the word into its subsequent categories—inner rings. Break these down further and further until you come up with a narrowed focus. This focus will allow both the reader and you, the writer, to target the topic.

The final portion of the introduction contains the presummary. This tells the readers specifically what they can expect to read. Using the television example, you might say that first you will cover the questionable educational benefits of television, second the insipid nature of television, and finally the harmful emotional effects that television has on children. Now you have better prepared your readers to follow you on a trip because now they have a preview of your topic. Further, with the presummary you help create a mindset within readers, preparing them for what comes next: the body—the evidence, the details.

THE BODY

The body represents the second section of the written document. Imagine that your thesis sits like a roof on several pillars. The pillars serve as the buttressed arguments that support the thesis. Each one of these pillars must relate directly back to the thesis you're trying to prove. The pillars themselves should be built from facts—the bricks and mortar that support them. In your TV document the pillars will be each of the three areas we discussed: the questionable educational effects of television; the insipidness of television; and finally the negative or hostile effects of television. Since each point derives from your thesis, the audience has a clear view of your objective up front. The readers can examine each one of these main points as you develop them.

Specifically, what supports the main points? A body of evidence forms the brick and the mortar for those pillars. You as the builder organize this information into logically written paragraphs, themselves constructed like minithemes (see chapter 7 for discussion on paragraph construction). Your paragraphs, in turn, support each pillar—main point—and, again, the main points support your thesis. Thus, you completely interweave the structure of your document for strength.

But what about the raw evidence you supply to build your paragraphs in the body of your paper? The weight of your supporting information (the evidence) comes in the form of statistics, when relevant and taken from reputable sources; quotations, again, when relevant to the topic and taken from known authorities; and testimony from those who should know, those considered to be experts. Personal experience can movingly illustrate a point, and personal testimony is effective if the source is particularly persuasive to readers.

You can organize the body's information (your evidence) in several ways. First, let's consider time chronology. Whenever you discuss a process, time sequence provides a good organizational structure for the body. We might say first A would happen, then B would occur, and finally C would happen. Or in 1964 television did...., in 1965 it was...., and in 1972.... Or on Monday a certain program appeared, on Thursday another program appeared, and on Saturday yet a third appeared. Another example uses time vertically within a day (e.g., at 9:00 A.M. a certain show came on; at 10:00 A.M. another one; at 3:00 P.M. another). Time chronologies work well in describing a process, or anything that involves time. Most writers who use the chronological approach usually start with the most distant date and then move toward the present. You can, however, start with the present and move backward.

The second type of structure you could employ is a spatial one, a particularly useful format when you must describe something tangible. Describing a place east or west, north or south, from the front to the back, or from the top to the bottom aids readers when you present a topic.

A third approach, the topical format, is widely used in informative writing and speaking. The television example provides a thesis sentence that contains several topics. It structures the body quite naturally. Using our television example, you would cover three thesis-related topics you covered in the presummary: the questionable educational impact of TV, its insipidness, and its hostile effects.

Remember that transitions help tie the body together into an understandable whole. Throughout the body you, as the writer, should tie the main points back to the thesis, thus weaving a tight structure. You can do this by employing specific transitional words that relate directly back to the thesis. For example, you might continue to thread back to your TV thesis by saying, "On the other hand, many people argue that television has its benefits." Words like *moreover, however, also, although*, and others (see chapter 7) help signal a shift of direction to readers while still maintaining a transitional flow. You can also employ pronouns. For example, you might refer to *television* at the end of one paragraph and then refer to *it* in the next. You can also achieve the same effect by using certain words in one paragraph and repeating them in the following one. Each of these transitional techniques serves to unify your writing, giving readers a holistic sense about the piece. Thus, your writing seems coherent, and therefore more believable.

THE CONCLUSION

Finally, after you have thoroughly developed your main points in the body, you need to sum up your points in a conclusion. First, you should restate your thesis for the readers. Restating the thesis in light of all the detail you've just given establishes a final and convincing overview for the readers. Next, hammer home the main points that supported your thesis so well. Now your readers can focus all of the evidence presented in the body back onto the thesis. You can do this by reviewing the main points, perhaps by commenting on them while restating the thesis. For example:

> Television has brought about many changes in our society, though not all of these societal changes have been good. Television has educated our children in certain rural areas, making it a mainstay of their education. Nonetheless, when examined closely, it is the main, and oftentimes specific, device that fosters illiteracy. Beyond that, recent studies seem to indicate that television may even incite violence in our increasingly violent society.

With the thesis restated and main points summarized, you offer a final statement that acts as an ending to the writing. Just as you had an opener, an attention-getter in your introduction, you ought to have some sort of closing statement. It can come in the form of statistics, quotes, references back to the opening statement, or any other method that will dramatically implant in the reader's mind the implications of what you've just said. In this particular case, perhaps you opened with a dramatic story about a prisoner on death row who said he had seen a murder on television and then copied it. You might want to refer back to him in a dramatic way, perhaps by saying that he still watches television.

STRUCTURE TO STAND ON

All documents need structure to stand on their own. That structure includes an introduction, a body, and a conclusion. When writers lace all three together with internal transitions and rhetorical devices, they provide the strength and unity that will hold any document together.

PROCESSWRITING WORKSHOP
REWRITING #8

Now that you've organized your paragraphs, it's time to structure your writing to make it easier for the reader to read. The old standby is appropriate here: tell them what you want to tell them; tell them; then tell them what you told them. It boils your paper down into three sections: the introduction, the body, and the conclusion.

Objectives

1. To organize a paper that the reader can easily comprehend.
2. To master the principles of a basic rhetorical structure.

Activities

Step 1

Choose an appropriate grabber for your paper. Now provide a statement about why your topic is important to the reader. Next, insert the thesis statement you developed earlier—it will give the reader some direction. Finally, tell the reader what aspects of the thesis you'll cover. Specifically state the direction the paper will take.

Step 2

Divide the body of the paper into three or four main points, each of which relate directly to the thesis. Organize the paragraphs and data from previous drafts and exercises to support each of these main points. It's like a pyramid: sentences support main points, and main points support the thesis.

Step 3

Finally, restate your thesis. Don't repeat it—restate it. Briefly summarize the main points. Finally, end your writing with a good closer. Look to the grabber techniques for ideas. Just make sure you bring the paper to a definite end.

Illustration

NOTE: Since this is a persuasive document, I am going to use a strong "need to know" grabber so the reader gets interested early on.

Step 1: Developing the Introduction

   According to a survey by American Instructors International, after one year of computerized training, most in-house training offices experience a 75 percent increase in the effectiveness of their instructors and efficiency of instruction. Computers are having an impact on every facet of American life, and training is no exception.

   I believe the percentage could be even higher in our Training Office because we have been plagued by a high turnover of instructors. Because of our antiquated office system, our instructors need between six months and a year to become fully operational. Worse, three former instructors who were interviewed for this study said they left the office primarily because they were frustrated by its inefficient systems. Turnover expenses have cost us approximately 25 percent of the budget each year.

   Computer expert Mary Jane Byte agrees that the solution to this problem is computerization. In fact, computerization of our training operation would increase both the effectiveness and efficiency of our training unit—two qualities that are looked at strongly by evaluators and auditors every two years.

How can this be done? The plan is simple: Through a computer system that includes different software applications, we can streamline the office system through computerized word processing, through an indexing and full-text retrieval system, through a database scheduling system, and through database instruction.

Step 2: Writing the Body of the Draft

We currently have a turnover problem in the training office caused by not enough secretarial support. All instructors are required to produce lesson plans for each one of their classes. Presently, with six instructors in the office, one secretary, and very limited typing support, the instructors are forced either to type on their own or use handwritten notes that only they can read. This causes problems such as loss of institutional memory when instructors leave. And over the last six years, six instructors have left, usually taking their lesson plans with them. According to Byte, having lesson plans on a word-processing disk file would allow new instructors to pull their lesson plans "off the shelf," thus preserving the historical/institutional memory of the office.

Word processing can also save money in the long run. Presently, we are considering hiring an additional secretary or clerk-typist, which would cost in excess of

$22,000 per year. The total estimate for computer software (programs) and hardware would be approximately $65,000, which would amortize typing costs in only three years.

New instructors must be able to access information and lesson plans on file quickly. Our current word-of-mouth retrieval program—where a new instructor goes to each person in the office for information—is hopelessly obsolete and inefficient. Also, the card-indexing system fell into disuse several years ago. Consequently, new instructors need an inordinate amount of time, oftentimes up to a year, to find out what is available, and even then they are only partially informed. To correct this problem, I suggest a full-text retrieval computer system. Such systems are available for under $1,000, and will not only produce an indexing system for all items in the file, but will also allow a full-text retrieval through key words. According to Byte, a package called "Quick-Find," which costs approximately $900, will suit our operation perfectly. Quick-Find produces full-text retrieval when words are entered that are contained in the text. Thus, if we entered the term **nonverbal,** we would get all the terms in all the lesson plans that refer to **nonverbal;** however, if we entered **nonverbal** and **hand gestures**, it would sufficiently limit the retrieval to only those references and lesson plans that include both those delineators. This capability would allow new instructors—and old ones—to focus closely on whatever issues are of interest to them.

As you know, our office works under complicated scheduling loads. Our six instructors are scheduled both on-site and off-site to suit the convenience of our executives. Also, we receive approximately thirty-five pieces of mail per day that need to be answered, dated, and time-recorded. Currently, we file incoming mail into a particular file with a notation as to the data of the outgoing communication, but we have no way to retrieve this information by name or by date. According to *Computer Match* magazine, June 1987, the software package "Schedule Master" can streamline our office system. This program, which sells for approximately $600, produces an easy-to-use, integrated retrieval system and scheduling system. Byte demonstrated that our secretary could be trained in three days to use this system. We expect its use would improve the efficiency in our office by 40 percent within the first year and by 50 percent within the next year. The savings would be up to $100,000 a year.

Hardware—We would need to buy approximately four data terminals: one computer terminal with memory, a hard disk drive and three dummy terminals. One would sit in my office; one at the secretary's desk; and the two others in the instructors' office area. All terminals would be used for entry and retrieval. A survey conducted by *Computer Match* magazine indicates that the most widely used computer in the training field is the ABC computer system. This computer hardware would cost $65,000.

Software—The three packages necessary are (1) the word-processing package ($700); (2) the indexing and full-text retrieval package, Quick-Find ($900); and (3) the scheduling/office management system, Schedule Master ($600). The total software costs would be $2,200.

Additional Training Software—The teaching of communications breaks down into two general areas: writing communications skills and public-speaking communications skills. Both these skills are "doing skills." They require hands-on training as well as drill and practice training.

In regard to hands-on training, a variety of exercises, particularly writing exercises, could be enhanced by a computer. According to Stallback (1980), drill and practice exercise using a computer in the classroom increases the efficiency of the trainer by at least 25 percent. Thus, by using drill-and-practice packages from ATM Software Inc., the trainer is relieved of purely mechanical responsibilities and can devote his time to more vital training. Also, more students can have more training in writing at the same time.

With respect to public speaking, two packages are available that review the fundamentals of speech as well as provide diagrams and drill and practice. Both packages are put out by the Real-Time Computer Software Company. They cost $500 apiece, but they can save approximately 10 to 15 percent of the teaching time in this course, because they can transmit basic knowledge to executives before they ever enter the classroom. One caveat mentioned by J. Sperling ("Enhancing the Effect of Training," *Communications Hotline* magazine) is that computer training must be integrated with teacher contact. Training exclusively with computers will not be nearly as efficient as integrating it with instructor contact. Therefore, all computer instruction, even at the prepresentation stage, would be integrated with teacher contact. Students would always be allowed to work solely on their own but not without some supervision and feedback of an instructor.

    I recommend that we demonstrate the equipment to the entire office and evaluate the software applications for training purposes.

Step 3: Writing the Conclusion

    My thesis is clear that efficiency and effectiveness can be improved by computer equipment. This effectiveness has been found in four other companies to date that I talked with. They are the Jones and Jones Training Corporation, the Smith and Smith Training Corporation, the XYZ Training Corporation, and the ABC Training Corporation. Each of these has experienced between a 30 and 40 percent level of efficiency in its training, and each sees greater prospects on the horizon. To quote from *Computer Match* magazine, "The training operation that does not use computers to assist it is using a 19th-century approach to a 21st-century problem."

9. TESTING

Now that you have joined your research to a solid structure, you should run up a trial balloon of your draft. You need to show your draft to readers to test them for a reaction. You will find it much easier to clear up ambiguities and miscues before, rather than after, you put your work in final form. As the word *testing* implies, this step of the writing process tests your draft on trusted readers who will give you honest feedback.

Think about it. You seek opinions and guidance all the time—when you buy a new dress, a suit, a car, or a boat. It always comforts you to know that you've not been blinded by your own immediate needs and desires.

In this chapter you will learn how to become a writing broker, how to form a writing support group, how to COACH others, and how to use experts to help your writing process.

THE WRITER-BROKER CONCEPT

People often envision a writer as someone who writes in a vacuum. They see a hermit-like figure huddled in a corner with a pen, typewriter, or computer—a solitary figure who interacts only with a piece of paper. Wrong! Writers come in all sizes, shapes, and personalities. And their methods of writing are just as diverse. Sure, writers go through much of the writing process alone. But writing, in fact, is not a solitary process for many, especially when they seek trial reactions from test readers. You need to adopt a writer-broker persona.

Writer-brokers function like all other brokers: they coordinate. Brokers bring things together, and most importantly, brokers shoulder the responsibility. Though writer-brokers can delegate any number of functions, in the end they must make the decisions—call the tough shots. So, while writers might ask for the opinions and advice of others, they choose to take or not take that advice. And when advice from others conflicts with your own ideas, decision making can be tough.

Nonetheless, a synergy, a power, comes from involving others in your writing. They can give you a different viewpoint, spot obvious flaws, tell you what works well, and tell you how they, as readers, reacted to your writing.

WRITING SUPPORT GROUPS

To get this reaction to and support for your writing, form your own writing support group. Members can be friends, coworkers, family, or any combination. What's important initially is to have an impartial observer read your writing and react to it. Moreover, the closer the group conforms to your selected audience, the more likely you are to get an accurate audience reaction.

How big should you make your group? Three to five people work well together. Any smaller and you get too little feedback; any larger and you rarely have enough control to get anything done. And how will you expect others to react? How would *you* react in the same circumstances?

THE COACH METHOD

Writing at its best reveals personal ideas. Once you write down your ideas, anyone can look at, inspect, and otherwise critique them—and by implication, *you*. Thus, when you react to another's writing or when others react to your writing, you should know how to react in a way that will not injure the writer's ego. To help you with this, just remember the word **COACH**: **c**ommend, **o**bserve, **a**sk, **c**onsider, **h**elp.

C — Commend

When you critique another's writing, always offer commendation (praise) first. Why? Because it helps build rapport by relieving the writer's anxiety. Remember, the writer's ego is at risk during the reaction period. If you make your initial remarks positive, the writer will breathe a sigh of relief, relax, and will listen to what you have to say. If, on the other hand, you begin with negative criticism, the writer will feel threatened and experience the fight-or-flight syndrome. First, the writer may fight: bristle and counterargue, explain, and get defensive. Or the writer will turn to flight: say nothing and wait for the earliest opportunity to bolt, to flee from the uncomfortableness of the session, never to return. In either case, communication between the reader and writer is significantly reduced or severed completely.

When you offer commendations, however, remember to be specific. Avoid generalizing, like, "Your paper was very interesting." Or, "You're doing such a great job." Most writers view these kinds of non-specific praises as hollow, meaningless, and even patronizing. A writer two hundred years ago called it "damning with faint praise."

Rather, you should specify exactly what pleases you. For example: "I like the way you clearly explained the function of the committee and how you offered concrete examples about their duties..." Or, "Your reasoning about the benefits of the XYZ project showed good, clear, sound logic, especially the part where you..." Note how specific praise presents the critic as a sincere and forthright person.

O — Observe

Next, always remain the objective observer. Sometimes you, as the reader, may not like or be interested in the topic. Nonetheless, you must serve as an interested observer for the writer's sake. To help do this, try mentally to role-play the "interested, intelligent ignorant." Imagine yourself as a reader who is generally intelligent, but ignorant about the specific subject. That way you remain open-minded. If you find that too hard, then try to discover something in the writing that you can link with your own life. Look for the positive benefits to yourself. Be an optimist whenever possible.

A — Ask

After building rapport with commendations and objective observations, you can begin to probe the writer with questions. Specifically, when you read a piece of writing and come across a confusing sentence or a place where things don't make sense, put a question mark. Then, at feedback time, pose these questions to the writer. Normally, the question itself will encourage many writers to reword or clarify the questionable writing. Questions normally don't threaten writers because questions aren't judgmental. Here are some examples of questions you might ask: "What did you mean when you wrote...?" "I don't quite understand the relationship between the two main characters. Can you explain it?" "Is there a reason you didn't give the background of the old policy before suggesting a new one?" "Will your targeted audience automatically understand what you mean by...?"

Notice how these questions get to the heart of weak points in the writing without necessarily attacking the writer.

C — Consider

Always consider the writer's feelings and intentions. As you already know, writing is an intensely personal endeavor. Writers get involved in their writing and, thus, their feelings come into play. Therefore, always take the softer approach—more considerate, more conservative, less radical—when critiquing someone's work.

H — Help

By this time, if you've used the COACH method, you've earned the right to offer direct help or criticism. Yes, you read correctly. You must *earn the right* to offer help. Sound crazy? Just think about how you use the same approach in your daily life. You'd never think of walking up to a stranger and telling him his tie and suit don't match, but you might tell that to a friend. Friends realize you've got their best interests at heart—even when you criticize.

Thus, after commending, observing, asking, and considering, you have earned the right to offer constructive help. Again, however, offer it in a considerate way: "I think you could make your paper even stronger if you rewrote this part." "I think your introduction was flawless but your conclusion needs a little more work to make it equal in force."

Remember, when offering criticism of any kind, you must first earn the right to do so—a gradual process at best. No blunt critique, no matter how accurate or well intentioned, will be received as well as criticism from those you trust.

EXPERT READERS

To ensure that the substance of your writing is correct, try to test your draft on an expert. For instance, if you're writing about bicycles, a bicycle expert should read your paper for substantive accuracy.

Do you want your bicycle expert to correct your grammar and spelling as well? No, for two reasons. First, your expert may know less than you about both writing and the mechanics of English. Second, faced with such a burden, your expert might duck very low to avoid the task. Such editing would intimidate even those experienced at it, let alone a technical expert who may have tried to avoid writing his or her entire life.

So, remove this burden of editing by letting your expert know up front that you want only to "rent" his or her technical brain for a few minutes. You might say, "Donna, I wonder if you would look over this paper and see if I've made any technical errors with respect to bicycles. Don't bother trying to correct the grammar or spelling. I just want your views on the subject matter." Such a preamble will relieve your expert of additional, unwanted responsibilities. It will allow her to do what she does best and to avoid what may well intimidate her.

By becoming a writer-broker and asking both your writing group and a technical expert to review your writing, you can be sure that you're on the right track. Now you're ready for a final proofreading.

PROCESSWRITING WORKSHOP
TESTING #9

As a writer, you need feedback before your target audience reads your final product. The testing step will get reactions, raise questions, and further clarify your paper. By getting reader reactions before you submit the final draft, you give yourself one last chance to revise it for your intended audience.

Objectives
1. To demonstrate the power of groups in revision (COACH method).
2. To show the value of expert readers.

Activities
Step 1

Call together your writing-process group. Give a copy of your draft to each member, then either read your draft aloud or ask them each to read it privately.

Now it's time for reader response, but first be sure to introduce your critics to the COACH rule system:
1. Commend—speak out about what works well.
2. Be objective—set aside personal biases.
3. Ask—question what you don't understand.
4. Be considerate—remember the author's feelings.
5. Help—offer suggestions and constructive comments to the author

Step 2

Offer your draft to any experts willing to read it. For instance, if the paper is about monetary problems, get an economist and a financial expert to look it over. Make sure they know you're only interested in their comments about your substantive ideas; you aren't looking for their help in grammatical editing.

Illustration

Step 1: Meeting with Your ProcessWriting Group

I've developed a small reader-writer group in my office. Both Jan and Dean are two coworkers I trust. We have agreed to share our drafts. We all adhere to the COACH system and understand that the critiques we give each other are to improve our writing. I gave a copy of my report to both and asked them to review it and give me their feedback. We sat down for about fifteen minutes after they had a chance to look at it. Here's how the meeting went:

First, they both complimented me on the amount of research I had done. Specifically, they liked the way I integrated opinions taken from written sources with oral comments made by the company expert, M. J. Byte. Because she is well respected by management, they thought her endorsement would add credibility to the project. Both generally added that they thought the project was worthwhile and plausible, and once again praised my foresight and ideas.

Next, they asked me a few questions. First, why didn't I include headers in the text to make it more readable? I told them I forgot and said I would add them in the next draft. Second, they asked if I had considered having a synopsis up front for the boss. I told them I considered it early on and just forgot it. Third, they asked if I wrote the last draft in two sections. They noted that while the writing in the first half was well done, it seemed to deteriorate somewhat as the memo went on. I admitted that I pushed to write the last part late at night and hadn't written it with as much care as the first section.

In sum, they suggested I introduce the memo with a synopsis, add headers, and edit the last part of the draft very closely. I thanked them for their comments and took their edited copies for later referral.

Step 2: Seeking Substantive Corroboration

I offered the same draft to Mary Jane Byte, our computer expert, to ask for her input. She advised that the computer hardware, which I had estimated at $65,000 based on an article from *Computer Match* magazine, would in fact probably cost only $50,000. She showed me various documents that supported this, and I changed my figure to $50,000.

10. ENDING

The time has come for you to finalize your piece of writing. If you've followed the process, you've spent considerable time with your writing, and by now you need invest only enough time for some final editing and proofing steps. Some simple strategies can help you clean up your writing, and this chapter lists a number of them for you. As you get more experienced, you'll develop your own editing and proofing strategies. But in the meantime, here are some that will get you started.

ALLOW TIME

Before you do a final reading, let your writing sit for as long as you can. Allowing time helps give you a much more objective eye. After you've been away from a piece of writing for a period of time, you'll be surprised at how objectively you can edit your own work.

READ YOUR WRITING ALOUD

To help you self-edit, always read your writing out loud. Wherever you falter during the reading, place a tick mark or wavy line and continue reading. Don't stop. Then, once you've finished the reading, go back to the spots you've marked. They usually will be the places where your writing needs revision.

Ideally, you should have someone read your writing aloud to you. You'll be amazed at how differently your writing sounds in another's voice. Problem areas seem to surface quickly and are easy to recognize. If no one is available to read, however, you might record yourself on tape, then play the recording and listen for hesitancies and inconsistencies in the reading. Once again, if you can allow time before replaying the recording, you'll be more objective and may even find that your voice sounds like that of a stranger.

USE THE ACTIVE VOICE

The passive voice has become almost the norm in business writing. Its use creates bloated and indirect language that is difficult for the reader to understand. For example: "The final plan *was approved* by the committee chairman and *was sent* forward to the executive vice president for his approval." This sentence contains more words than necessary, and its passive construction leaves the reader wondering who sent the program to the vice president. Note what happens if you edit this and put it in the active voice: "Tom Jones, the committee chairman, *approved* the final plan and *sent* it to the executive vice president for his approval." Now the sentence is clear and so is the responsibility.

Review your writing and look for either implied or direct use of the passive voice. To help you spot the passive voice, note all the by's in your writing. They usually indicate that a passive construction lurks nearby. Then, recast the sentence in the active voice, and see how it makes a stronger, more direct sentence that the reader can more easily comprehend.

AVOID THE VERB "IS"

Like the passive voice, the verb *is* or *to be*, in all of its forms, creates weak writing. *Is*, like the other so-called linking verbs (*appear, become, seem, feel, grow, act, look, taste, smell, sound*), merely links subjects with adjectives or objects and avoids any action. On the other hand, strong, active verbs add life to any sentence. Thus, too many linking verbs will cut out the life and dilute the power of your writing.

> *Dull*: The dog appeared happy when he saw the young boy. The boy was young and cute and acted like a typical boy as he got off the bus.

> *Alive:* The dog vigorously wagged his tail, eagerly awaiting the boy. The eight-year-old blond-haired boy jumped off the bus, chasing a friend while yelling at the top of his lungs.

The second sentence allows you to picture in your mind a loving dog waiting for his lively young master. The first sentence leaves you flat; you can't "see" any picture. By using active verbs, you help the reader see the action: *wagged, jumped, yelling*—all help the writing come alive. Admittedly, the adjectives placed next to the nouns also help, but the verbs create the action, something your mind's eye picks up naturally.

USE SHORT SENTENCES— THE RULE OF TWENTY

Look at any piece of writing, and if you see more than three lines of typing without a period or semicolon, chances are you'll start getting confused. More than twenty words in a sentence leads to reader confusion. So reread what you've written, note with a wavy line in the margin where you see lengthy sentences, and go back to revise them. There are several ways to trim excess writing fat: cut prepositional phrases, look for restatements that add nothing to your writing, and, again, avoid the passive voice.

Cut prepositional phrases like along the lines of, as of this date, at the present time, and in the event that; instead, use like, today, now, and if. Locate a prepositional phrase, and ask yourself if you can use one word where you've written three. Whenever you see the preposition *of,* see if you can use the possessive to eliminate a couple of words:

Bloated: The meeting was held in the office of the president.

Trimmed: The meeting was held in the president's office.

You also can trim language by looking for obvious restatements or for words that have a double meaning:

Duplicative: The staffers got together and did some advance planning; that is, they put their heads together to find solutions.

Efficient: The staffers met and planned strategies.

Finally, look again for the passive voice. A prepositional phrase usually introduces it, and by eliminating the phrase you can trim back the sentence:

Passive: The market is dictated by the large investors.

Active: Large investors affect the market.

The first sentence contains eight words, the second only five—that's a large savings in words.

DON'T SMOTHER VERBS

Don't camouflage verbs, or you'll lose the action and flavor of your sentences. To clean up hidden verbs, try this tip: underline words ending with *-ent, -ant, -ion, -ment, -ence, -ance,* or *-ency.* Writers frequently place these endings on verbs to make them nouns, thereby destroying their action:

Hidden: The instructor made the standing assignment for implementation of better productivity of students.

Clear: The instructor assigned regular homework to ensure student productivity.

Notice that when you eliminate muffled words, like *assignment* and *implementation*, the sentence shortens and comes alive.

USE CONCRETE LANGUAGE

Abstract language continually creeps into corporate writing. Vague, imprecise language paints a fuzzy picture. You can paint a crystal-clear picture by asking yourself the old standby questions: who, what, when, where, why, and how?

> ***Fuzzy:*** The supervisor of one of our units possesses the proper skills to navigate a navigational vehicle.

> ***Clear:*** Our contracts manager can fly planes.

Notice how the second sentence gets right to the meat of the issue, letting you know who can do what. Also, remember the KIS principle: keep it simple.

KEEP RELATED WORDS TOGETHER

Misplaced modifiers cause readers heartburn. They have to reread to figure out what you're trying to say, or worse, they misunderstand:

> ***Misplaced:*** After months of traveling, the secretary met with her boss at the airport.

> ***Clearer:*** After months of traveling, the boss met his secretary at the airport.

Notice that in the first sentence you may have thought the secretary was doing all the traveling. Not so. It was the boss's homecoming.

To eliminate this common problem, always place the modifier—adverb or adjective, even prepositional phrase (when acceptable)—nearest the word it modifies.

> ***Foggy:*** The boss discussed the problem in the men's room.

> ***Clearer:*** In the men's room the boss discussed the problem.

By moving the prepositional phrase you change the meaning of the sentence. After all, the problem was not in the men's room—it was only discussed there.

Avoid Shifts

Avoid shifts in number, tense, sex, subject, or point of view.

Number

Subjects should always match their verbs and pronouns. Plural subjects take plural verbs and pronouns:

> ***Mixed numbers:*** The engineer asked if they could come in the room to perform their tests.

> ***In line:*** The engineer asked if he could come in the room to perform his tests.

Tense

Shifting verb tenses also confuses readers:

Time problem: The supervisor viewed the dispute and breaks it up.

On time: The supervisor saw the fight and broke it up.

Sex

Beware the sex-biased words in your writing. Certain titles or words deny women the stature they deserve. Avoid male-dominated titles, like policeman and workman, in favor of more generic terms: police officer or worker. To avoid sex-biased language use plural subjects:

Not: Each worker took off his hard hat.

But: The workers took off their hard hats.

Whatever strategy you use in your writing, avoid sexist language whenever possible.

Subject

Changing the subject in midsentence throws the reader off course. Avoid any shift in subject when possible:

Not: The copy editor finished the document, and it was rewritten.

But: The copy editor finished the document, then she had it rewritten.

DETERMINE POINT OF VIEW

The point of view gives the reader a perspective of who is telling the story. Some people write memos and reports from an "I" or first-person perspective; others write them from a "you" or second-person perspective (like this book); and still others write from a "he, she, or they" or third-person perspective. Each perspective is the point of view, and shifting it in your writing confuses readers:

Not: The manager said that when I read the memo, you could see the mistakes that we had made.

But: The manager said that when he read the memo, he could see the mistakes.

MAKE YOUR WRITING READABLE

White space is that blank area on a printed page. White space provides eye relief to the reader. Pick up most single-spaced legal documents, for example, and you'll usually find very little white space—little eye relief. As a result, readers tend to avoid such documents. When was the last time you took out your life insurance policy or the deed to the house and read it for pleasure?

By creating white space in a piece of writing you make it more readable and, thus, it will be read more often. Also, if well formatted with white space, your document will look more organized, leaving a much better impression on the reader—and that is important in business.

To create white space and to order your writing, try these tips:

- Indent main points.
- Underline to stress a point.
- Use bullets and lists.
- Always double space, but if you must single space, skip two lines between paragraphs.
- Design short paragraphs.
- Break up text with illustrations.
- Break space and provide shifts in the text with liberally used subheadings.
- Number items in lists or number major points you want to make.

LETTING GO

Finally, after you have finished all your work—after you and your group, or friend, have proofed and reproofed your writing—it's time to submit it and wait for the results. Once you have finished your piece of processwriting, don't be surprised if you feel a little down. When you invest so much of yourself in anything, you will have a hard time letting it go. Many business people feel somewhat depressed when they complete a particularly long document. It's been such a big part of them for so long. What's the cure? Start writing something new. Good luck!

ENDING

PROCESSWRITING WORKSHOP
ENDING #10

Now it's time to check your paper for mechanics. You've held off doing this until now to save time. Check for spelling, punctuation, grammar, and format. When you're done, submit it and end the process.

Objective

To prepare a final document for submission.

Activities

Step 1:

First, reread chapter 10 in this book. Note all the tips. Now go through your draft, using these tips to make sure you have used direct, useful verbs; kept sentences short; avoided abstractions; kept related words together; not shifted number, tense, sex, subject, or point of view; and used solid construction in your writing.

Read your draft out loud, and into a tape recorder if you have one. Wherever you stumble, put a pencil check, but don't stop reading. When you're done, go back to the spots you checked. Chances are good that those pencil-marked places will show up problems in your writing.

Step 2
A job well done—Congratulations!

Illustration
Step 1: Memorandum Report—Final

TO: Joan Jones, Director of Training   8/7/87

FROM: Raymond Stark, Chief of Communication Instruction Office

SUBJECT: COMPUTER ENHANCEMENTS TO COMMUNICATION INSTRUCTIONS TO IMPROVE EFFICIENCY AND EFFECTIVENESS

Report Synopsis

We currently have an inefficient training system in our Communication Instruction Office. Turnover of instructors, a lack of typists, a lack of full-text retrieval systems, and no effective drill-and-practice methods—all are causing a noticeable decrease in the efficiency and effectiveness of the office. Documented research shows that computerization could increase our efficiency by 25 percent. Computers can improve our operation in several areas: word processing, scheduling, and database instruction. According to M. J. Byte, the company computer expert, our initial cost outlay for a computer system will be paid off in only two years.

Details

According to a survey by American Instructors International, after one year of computerized training, most in-house training offices experience a 25 percent increase in the effectiveness of their instructors and in the efficiency of their instruction. Computers are having an impact on every facet of American life, and training is no exception.

I believe the increase in efficiency could be even greater in our Training Office because we have been plagued by a high turnover of instructors. Because of our antiquated office system, our instructors need between six months and a year to become fully operational. Worse, three former instructors who were interviewed for this study said they left the office primarily because they were frustrated by its inefficient systems. Turnover expenses have cost us approximately 25 percent of the budget each year. Computer expert Mary Jane Byte agrees that the solution to this problem is computerization. In fact, computerization of our training operation would increase both the effectiveness and efficiency of our training unit—two qualities that are looked at strongly by evaluators and auditors every two years.

How can this be done? The plan is simple: We can streamline the office system with a computer system that includes different software applications: word processing, an indexing and full-text retrieval system, a scheduling system, and database instruction.

Word Processing System

We currently have a turnover problem in the training office caused by not enough secretarial support. All instructors are required to produce lesson plans for each one of their classes. Presently, for six instructors in the office, we have only one secretary and very limited typing support. The instructors, therefore, are forced either to type on their own or use handwritten notes that only they can read. This system causes obvious problems, such as loss of institutional memory when instructors leave. And over the last six years, six instructors have left—taking their lesson plans with them. According to Ms. Byte, a word processor would allow new instructors to pull their lesson plans "off the shelf," thus preserving the historical/institutional memory of the office.

Word processing will save a lot of money in the long run. Presently, we are considering hiring an additional secretary or clerk-typist, which would cost in excess of $22,000 per year. The total estimate for computer software (programs) and hardware would be approximately $50,000, which would nearly amortize typing costs in only two years. Specific details regarding computer costs will be printed later in this report.

Indexing and Full-Text Retrieval

New instructors must be able to access information and lesson plans quickly. Our current word-of-mouth retrieval program—where a new instructor goes to each person in the office for information—is hopelessly obsolete and inefficient. Also, our card-indexing system fell into disuse several years ago. Consequently, new instructors need an inordinate amount of time, oftentimes up to a year, to find out what is available. Even then they are only partially informed.

To correct this problem I suggest a full-text retrieval computer system. Such systems are available for under $1,000. In addition to producing an indexing system for all items in the file, they also allow a full-text retrieval through keywords. According to Ms. Byte, a software package called "Quick-Find," which costs approximately $900, will suit our operation perfectly. Quick-Find produces full-text retrieval when words are entered that are contained in the text. Thus, if we entered the term **nonverbal,** we would get all the references in all the lesson plans which use **nonverbal**; however, if we entered **nonverbal** and **hand gestures**, it would sufficiently limit the retrieval to only those references and lesson plans that include both those delineators. This capability would allow new instructors—and old ones—to focus closely on whatever issues are of interest to them.

Office Management Scheduling System

As you know, our office works under complicated scheduling loads. Our six instructors are scheduled to teach both on-site and off-site to suit the convenience of our executives. Also, we receive approximately thirty-five pieces of mail per day that need to be answered, dated, and tracked. Currently, we have no way to retrieve mail information by name or by date. According to *Computer Match* magazine, June 1987, the software package "Schedule Master" can streamline our office system. This program, which sells for approximately $600, produces an easy-to-use, integrated retrieval and scheduling system. Ms. Byte demonstrated that our secretary could be trained in three days to use this system. We expect its use would improve the efficiency of our office by 10 percent within the first year and by 20 percent within the next year. The savings would be up to $100,000 in the years to come. Further, the quality of communication instruction would significantly improve.

Database Instruction

Our teaching of communications breaks down into two major general areas: writing communications skills and public-speaking communications skills. Both of these skills are "doing skills." They require hands-on training as well as drill-and-practice training. For the hands-on training, a variety of exercises, particularly writing exercises, could be enhanced by a database instruction computer. For example, according to Stallbach (1980), drill-and-practice computer exercises in the classroom increase the efficiency of the trainer by at least 10 percent. Thus, by using a drill-and-practice database instruction package, which is provided by ATM Software Inc., New Jersey, more students can receive more training with decreased drain on instructors. The instructors, therefore, will have more time to give individual help to those who need it.

Two database instruction packages are available that review the fundamentals of speech and provide drill and practice for oral communications. These packages are marketed by the Real-Time Computer Software Company and cost $500 apiece. I estimate they can save approximately 10 to 15 percent of the teaching time in our public-speaking course, and can give executives foundation knowledge of the subject before ever coming to class. One caveat mentioned in J. Sperling's article, "Enhancing the Effect of Training," in the *Communications Hotline* magazine is that computer training must be integrated with teacher contact. Exclusive computer training will not be nearly as effective as computer training coupled with instructor training. Therefore, we would never use these packages as replacements for our teacher-based training.

Purchasing Needs

To meet our computer needs, we would need to buy approximately four data terminals: one computer terminal with a hard disk drive and three dummy terminals that operate off the main terminal. One terminal would sit in my office; one at the secretary's desk; and the two others in the instructors' office area.

All terminals would be used for entry and retrieval. A survey conducted by *Computer Match* magazine indicates that the most widely used computer in the training field is the ABC computer system. This computer hardware would cost $50,000.

Software—The three packages necessary are (1) the word-processing package ($700); (2) the indexing and full-text retrieval package, Quick-Find ($900); and (3) the scheduling/office management system, Schedule Master ($600). The total software costs would be $2,200.

Recommendation

Computer equipment will clearly improve the efficiency and effectiveness of our office operations. In fact, I have found four other training companies that have tested the value of a similar system: the Jones and Jones Training Corporation, the Smith and Smith Training Corporation, the XYZ Training Corporation, and the ABC Training Corporation. All of these have experienced between a 30 and 40 percent growth level of efficiency in their training—and see greater prospects on the horizon. To quote from *Computer Match* magazine, "The training operation that does not use computers is no longer viable—it is using a 19th-century approach to solve a 21st-century problem." Therefore, I recommend purchasing the equipment outlined in this memo as soon as the budget process allows.

About the Author

Steve Gladis is an FBI Agent and is also the editor of the *FBI Law Enforcement Bulletin,* the most widely read law enforcement magazine in the world. Most recently Mr. Gladis served as the chief of speechwriting at the FBI, and as an instructor at the FBI Academy he taught public speaking and writing courses in the National Academy Program. Also an adjunct professor at the University of Virginia, Mr. Gladis holds a B.A. degree in English from Providence College, an M.A. in Writing and Editing (English) from George Mason University (GMU), and is currently a Doctor of Arts in Education candidate at GMU, concentrating on the teaching of writing and curriculum development. He is the author of numerous magazine articles and has previously published two books entitled *Survival Writing* and *Survival Communication* (Kendall/Hunt). Mr. Gladis lives in Virginia with his wife Donna and his two children Kimberly and Jessica.